Praise for THE ABUNDANCE LEAGUE

"I want you to read this book, in part because it is such a compelling read, and in part because there is so much wisdom in these pages, so many observations about how people think, how they interact, how their passions move them, and also how their passions betray them. *The Abundance League* is that rare story collection that helps you look at those you know, and those you may just glimpse, with new insight—and also entertains you along the way. I am just of blown away by how much intelligence about people it contains."

-- Robin Black (author of *Life Drawing* and *If I Loved You I Would Tell You This*)

*   *   *

"In *The Abundance League*, Larry Loebell delves into seemingly ordinary moments and uncovers surprising layers in the deep. The ten stories in this collection are populated with watchers and listeners and, again and again, small, acute observations that yield big truths. These are my favorite kind of stories: honest, free of gimmicks, written with urgency, clarity and insight."

-- Elise Juska (author of *The Hazards of Sleeping Alone, Getting Over Jack Wagner,* and *The Blessings*)

"This short story (*49 Seconds in the Box*) is a little heartbreaker. The narrator, Mira, gets in the elevator on the way home after having her beloved dog, Jake, put to sleep. She reflects on all those many trips up and down with Jake, and we learn that she counted the moments of his dying as she's counted the time in the elevator over the years. This is a concise, wise story that works by juxtaposing the anti-dog Arnie (who cares for his dying wife) with the dog-loving Mira, who has had to dispatch her love. There isn't a wasted word in here."

-- Bonnie Jo Campbell (author of *Mothers Tell Your Daughters* and *Once Upon a River*), on choosing *49 Seconds in the Box* as a finalist for the 2015 Marguerite McGlinn National Prize for Fiction.

The Abundance League

Stories

Larry Loebell

Shelley —
Enjoy!
Larry Loebell
4/1/17

Blue Footed Books
Philadelphia   2016

ISBN-13:
978-0692679593 (Blue Footed Books)

Blue Footed Books
614 South Eighth Street # 373
Philadelphia, PA 19147
TheAbundanceLeague@BlueFootedBooks.com

THE PERFECT DAY

The shock of learning about the suicide drew Anton back to the previous day and to his assumptions and misapprehensions about the dead man. He had certainly seen the man on the beach yesterday, during the free hour after lunch. Determined to work on his tan, Anton had walked to the ocean, stretched out on a towel, and dozed on and off until a strong shift in the breeze blew a swirl of sand across his face. At the same moment, a spray of mossy seawater drifted in his direction, propelled skyward by the breakers crashing a few yards from where he lay. A fine drizzle fell on him as if shaken from an aspergillum. But neither the spray nor the sand would have roused Anton more than momentarily had not a child's squeal reached his ear simultaneously. It was the sound's sharpness that destroyed his drowsy peace, caused him to open his eyes and turn toward the water.

Of the few people in the ocean, the two closest to Anton were the man and a young girl swimming between the safety flags. The girl was the only child in the water. She and the man were midway between where the surf petered out on the sand and the furthest swimmers from shore. The man was standing, chest deep, in a trough between waves. The girl was riding on a tightly inflated rubberized raft, the kind displayed by size in racks in front of every tourist shop across the highway. It was similar in style to one he had refused to buy his own children earlier in the summer on a day trip to Coney Island, knowing they would have used it

1

for five minutes and then abandoned it for something else. Though the girl and her raft seemed to be bobbing like a buoy on an anchor, the man was actually guiding her, pressing down on her ankles to raise the nose of the float over the incoming swells. With each wave the girl skimmed over, Anton now realized, she expelled another squeal.

Anton rolled slightly, freed his arm from under his head, and checked his watch. There were sessions starting in the ballroom in twenty minutes. He needed to return to his room to change, but he was not quite ready to quit the beach. He and his wife had come down from New York for this conference at no little expense, and he'd be damned if he was not going to relax and enjoy himself between sessions. The conference, a gathering of advertising agency account executives, had become a yearly event since the war, but Anton missed the last one because he caught a particularly nasty summer grippe that had utterly flattened him. His wife, his second wife, had been annoyed to miss that conference because she had already purchased a gown for the annual award banquet, at which Anton was supposed to have been honored for his work on the Whitman Sampler Celebrity campaign. Summer formals were a trial to shop for, his wife had told him, especially given that a gown for events in warmer winter resort getaways was not the same as a gown for actual summer wear in New York. But she had found a perfect dress, in robin's egg blue, with spaghetti straps and a low neckline. It showed her off well, the saleswoman in Bergdorf's had told her, meaning it flattered her bust line, and she agreed. Anton knew all of this because his wife had repeated the conversation practically verbatim when she modeled the gown at home. Very slightly risqué, perhaps, for her set in New York, but hardly even an eyebrow-raiser for crossing the ballroom at a resort hotel like this one, where typical lobby dress was a bathing suit, open-toed sandals, and a short terrycloth robe. Now, a year later, she was determined to wear it, even though she worried it might be

2

deemed, by the fashionable wives of the other men, a style that was somewhat old hat.

The panel that Anton was interested in attending was discussing marketing products to children. Some recent market analysis had suggested children might be influencing adult buying habits for certain types of products, breakfast cereals and clothing particularly, to a greater degree than anyone had imagined. And there was talk, though many of his peers discounted it, that televisions, which had barely reached, at the beginning of the current year, a two-percent penetration of all American homes, were about to drop in price and could perhaps become as significant an influence on people as radio or newspapers. His own children, ages six and eight, had seemed mesmerized by a television they saw at Holcomb's, the local furniture store, but they were at an age when anything flashy or new seemed to hold their attention for a little while.

His children's faces came briefly to mind as they had looked in the changing bluish light from that screen, sitting cross-legged on the floor in front of a row of curious adults who stood behind them in the aisle of the store, also gawking. Now his children were in Maine, where their mother, his first wife, was vacationing for the month. They would not have been tolerant of any activity that required them to be as trusting of an adult playmate as the girl on the raft riding the waves seemed to be, especially if that playmate was one of their parents. Or perhaps, he thought, it was just that his children simply did not trust him. They seemed perpetually distracted when they were with him every other weekend. They were resistant to suggestions, impervious to his enthusiasm. Even when he was able to capture their attention, cheerlead their participation in some activity, their interest seemed to quickly flag. He rarely felt that his ideas for activities squared with their interests, though he could not seem to figure out what would.

Anton had doubts that television could generate the kind of interest its promoters promised, and though his own restless kids seemed becalmed by it, he wondered whether they would have become bored with it a moment or two later. But because his colleagues saw promise in it, he was determined to attend the session to assure himself his firm was at least up on the latest.

Sitting up, he watched the man and the girl playing in the waves. Focusing on her now, he realized he had seen the girl the day before, in the lobby bar he thought, with her mother, though it had been the woman and not the child he really recalled. Someone in his group had known the woman and invited her to join them. He was sure he had heard her name, but he did not remember it. Other than brand names and people he forced himself to remember for business, Anton's retention of names was hit and miss. People's information simply didn't stick to him, though he liked to believe he never forgot a face. Whoever it had been in his crowd who called the woman over also said *sotto voce* that her husband was arriving later. Anton remembered wondering if this meant her husband was joining her later at the bar or had not yet arrived at the hotel. Now he wondered if there had been another intention in the fact that the information about the husband had been whispered. He wondered now if any of the other men had heard the suggestion that the child's mother was available, or perhaps that the whisperer had already experienced some kind of intimacy with her.

The girl, who had not precisely been with the woman at first, arrived belatedly at her side, sidling up to her and poking her on the leg, just hard enough to get a reaction, with the nearly foot-long stick of an all-day sucker. The oversized lollypop had once had a face on it, but the features were now a lipstick and saffron colored smear. The candy had been presented to every child at check-in, at the same time a rose was presented to welcome each woman, a sugary gift that

4

had registered with Anton as foolish the minute he had seen it, though he knew his own kids would have loved getting something like that. His ex-wife had forbidden him to give them candy so of course sweets in all their forms became objects of intense desire.

The woman, carrying a wicker bag filled with towels and sand toys, reacted to the child's jab at her leg, jerking slightly as if she had been shocked by electricity, spilling a splash of martini on her terrycloth drape. This image was clear to him. He was a visual guy; that's what they said of him at the agency. What Anton retained about the moment with absolute clarity was the rise of the woman's chest as she reacted to the child's mild assault, and how the woman's hand, still encumbered by the basket of beach toys, rose instinctively to touch the spill. And he remembered now that the woman had laughed, and made a self-deprecating comment to the men around her at the bar, before kneeling and turning her attention – and scowl – to the girl.

The man with the girl on the beach must be the formerly missing husband, the father of the girl, Anton decided. But then he looked familiar too, and Anton was certain he had seen him already in the hotel, perhaps even before he had been told at the bar that the husband was absent. He looked like the man he had noticed at the concierge's desk in the lobby the night before, and considered this for a moment before deciding that he must simply be mistaken. Clearly the man with the girl in the ocean was the girl's father, now arrived. Who else would he be?

Anton watched the man and the girl for only another moment before turning to look at the hotel. Eleven stories tall, a hundred and thirty luxury rooms, six hundred feet of private beach, two all-weather tennis courts, sundecks, and air conditioning, it was exactly as described in the brochure, and in all of its particulars, the perfect place for a conference of successful advertising men.

But Anton knew it was the bars that really mattered. Where business was really done. Where deals were made. Where tidbits of information changed hands that shaped the way business was transacted in his profession, and thereby, he knew without getting too grandiose about it, but without false modesty either, shaped the country, the future, the world. Anton adjusted his position to look at the beach bar, but discovered there was only one person there in the midday heat. He shaded his eyes and squinted, trying to figure out if the solitary drinker was anyone he knew. At a different hour of the day, one less brutally spotlighted in the sun's glare, when the bar was more crowded with refugees from either beach or conference rooms, those gathered there would look, from his vantage, like they had stepped out of a Noel Coward play, a tableau of spot-lit gestures, glasses, and cigarettes. At least that's what it had seemed to him yesterday when he and his wife strolled by in the late afternoon. Now, as Anton studied the lone man at the bar, he recognized him as the fellow who had been on his marlin charter the day before, a barrel-chested Texan who now worked in Atlanta, and whose idea of casual attire was dungarees, a checked shirt, and a Stetson hat. An ad man, like himself, but without the polish or style New Yorkers cultivated to be admitted to the offices of corporate executives and their moneyed lawyers and accountants, this man was gruff; he had nearly lost a rod when he refused to let the medium-sized blue fin he had managed to hook run itself tired. He fought it, cowboy style, trying to bring it in without exhausting it first – a bad strategy. He swore and worked the rod, but eventually the fish tore free, leaving a parcel of skin hanging on the triple-barbed hook like a bloody flag. After watching him, Anton decided he did not like the man, did not like Texans in general, and definitely didn't like marlin fishing. When the man signaled broadly for another drink, the bartender reacted slowly, probably hoping he could close up for a while until things cooled down. Other than the Texan, the bar was deserted. At this hour, with temperatures nearing their daily peak, the action, Anton knew, had moved inside where there was air conditioning.

As he worked on rousing himself enough to stand and walk back up the beach to get ready for his session, he realized that the man and girl had left the water. She was running now, full tilt, toward the hotel. Anton studied her. She was a long-legged child and her strides were almost leaps, her bathing suit bright above her pale legs. Her feet kicked up sand behind her – perhaps she was making this happen intentionally – though she seemed to be running with the unbridled lack of self-awareness that children who do not know they are being watched exhibit before the world inflicts inhibition on them. When she vanished into the shadow the hotel cast onto the sand, he shifted his attention to the man, who walked up the beach in the same direction, carrying the rubber raft under his arm at an angle that brought it awkwardly into contact with his stomach and chest. Anton sized him up, calculated he was on the tall side. He moved neither swiftly nor slowly, but ambled across the beach as if his exact destination had not yet occurred to him, but when it did he knew he had all the time in the world to get there. Anton was not surprised that the child who had seemed so delighted to be with him a moment before, now seemed to have abandoned him without even a backward glance. His own children had certainly done the same thing to him.

After the man had disappeared into the shadow of the hotel as well, Anton rose, gathered his towel and walked up the beach, using his towel as he walked to mop sweat and sand off of his face, arms, and chest.

It was late afternoon before news of the man's suicide spread through the ranks of the ad men. Anton and his colleagues gathered in the bar before dinner and compared what they had heard. He was not one of them, not there for their conference, of that they were certain. The hotel staff

7

had let it be known, lest there be panic, that the gunshot was self-inflicted. They did not want anyone to think a deranged man with a gun was stalking hotel guests, though deranged was certainly what Anton and some of his colleagues concluded anyway. Someone said the man had been on his honeymoon, that he had been in the service in the European Theater of Operations during the war, had been wounded and had suffered a long recovery. Someone else said he had been some sort of celebrity, a musician they thought. Anton was skeptical of all these details, suspicious that anyone could know this much of the dead man's history in such short order. Someone said that they thought he had been in the lobby bar the night before, and someone else said they had seen him buying a frankfurter for a child in the poolside cafe. There was a rumor that his wife had been asleep in the room at the time he pulled the trigger, and there was debate about whether it was forgivable, even assuming he had some sort of mental defect or disease, that he had done such a horrible thing in the presence of his wife. If indeed he had done it. The Texan from the marlin charter had the most salacious tidbit. He said he had talked to the chambermaid who had tried to console the wife, and that as far as the chambermaid was concerned it was not at all clear who had done it. The chambermaid, the Texan informed them, suspected the wife, which he insisted made complete sense given that, as far as he was concerned, the most dangerous people on the planet were jealous women with guns. Without directly dismissing the murder theory or confronting its vocal proponent, the ad men focused back on the prevailing view, agreeing that if it was suicide, it was the worst thing one person could do to another. The conversation flagged after that, and Anton used the excuse of needing to shower and shave before dinner to make his getaway.

Back in his room, Anton discovered that the phone lines, which had been fairly jammed before the news of this death spread through the hotel, were impossible to access after it. He tried calling his office in New York several times, only to be told by the hotel operator that call volume was unusually high, and that it might take an hour or more before there would be a free circuit and his call could be put through. He told the operator to forget it; nothing he had to say was that important.

Soon Anton's wife arrived. She had been sunbathing at the pool. She knew a bit more about the suicide than he did. The man was here with his wife, she told him, and they were on their honeymoon. Someone had spoken to her about it. When Anton asked if they had children his wife scowled at him. They were newlyweds, she reminded him, and hardly likely to have children. Anton's wife told him she heard the man's wife had been sleeping, and apparently was awakened at the sound of the gunshot to the scene of her husband's bloody action.

At first, it had not occurred to Anton that the man he saw on the beach holding the ankles of the girl on the float could be the same man who now occupied the attention of virtually all of the hotel's guests. Nor had he been aided in making the connection when he was told that the man who had shot himself had no children. He only began to contemplate this mystery after he saw the child he had seen in the water crossing the lobby with her mother while he and his wife were headed to dinner. The girl was holding hands with a man to whom her resemblance was unmistakable. Only then did Anton realize he must have been mistaken about the relationship between the man he had seen in the water and the child. Nor did either mother or child crossing the lobby seem grief-stricken to him. Did they even know, he wondered? Had they been out together, swimming or beachcombing when the tragedy unfolded? They were dressed in swimming gear. Anton wondered if the woman even knew that her daughter had been swimming with the man he saw on the beach, or if, in the way of childhood, she had somehow adopted him for a time, made a friend for a moment, and then, out of his presence, had simply ceased to think about him as mattering to her at all. People came and went all the time in childhood; knowing who was important and who was not was an adult skill. An acquired skill. After Anton's own father left, his mother had lots of friends, though few of them had stayed around very long. One or two had tried to enlist him in the cause of making his mother a more permanent fixture in their lives. He had been taken to a few ball games, a few traveling fairs set up on vacant lots behind one or another church in his neighborhood. Someone took him fishing. Someone took him ice-skating. He had liked some of the men, but now he couldn't recall a single name or face. His own children occasionally mentioned visitors who came to see his ex-wife, talking to him as if he would surely know who the men were, which, of course, he did not. He did sometimes conjure them, these men his children innocently reported were courting his ex-wife, when he wrote his alimony and child support check, wondering if she would remarry and relieve him of the burden of supporting her. Despite the children, his ex-wife was probably still considered somewhat of a catch, though he wondered if remarriage was even what she wanted.

Even if the parents of the child he had seen swimming with the man knew the man, and even if the girl asked about him by name, or was curious about his sudden absence from her world, or from the world at large if she could imagine that, Anton assumed that her parents would not make a big deal of it. Why traumatize the girl, Anton thought. Why expose her, at her age, to the kind of internal unhappiness that could make such a thing happen? If unhappiness it was.

As they got dressed for dinner, Anton's wife told him that she hoped the shock of the man's death would not undermine their vacation, or the high spirits of the conventioneers. It was bad enough that the man's poor wife had to suffer. But the question lingered for Anton. Why had

10

this man been with the girl on the beach if he wasn't her father?

It was his wife who pointed out the dead man was, in fact, the same person they had seen in the lobby talking to the concierge the night before. It troubled Anton that he had allowed himself to easily dismiss what he had clearly remembered accurately, temporarily remaking what he knew to be true on the basis of his misunderstanding of the relationship between the child swimming in the ocean and the man. But what were they to each other? He could not shake the sense that in assuming the man was the child's father, and seeing their apparent comfort playing together in the ocean, he had missed something essential, something he should not have missed, about each of them, something that might have been in plain view, if he had either trusted his recollection or focused on it. Convinced that he had seen the man not once but twice in the past two days, he told his wife that he could not help but wonder if there had been something someone might have done, some foretelling in the man's carriage or actions that might have been a clue to his intentions. Anton's wife reminded him that if the man's wife did not see this coming, it was unlikely anyone else would have. People are a mystery, she told him. But Anton wondered if he agreed with her. His occupation and the occupations of all the people gathered at the hotel with him for this conference, assumed that behavior was anything but mysterious. Buying habits, social habits, how people chose things, what they wanted, how they would act – these things were predictable. Within a small margin of error, for adults, certainly, he believed things could be known.

At dinner, after a decision had been made by the organizers of the conference to continue their events, there was abstract talk about the value of life, about its cheapness and preciousness, about the choice to take one's own life, about what one could or could not know about the state of mind of another. There was sympathy all around for the man's wife, varying degrees of sympathy and blame for the man, talk about his pain, about the selfishness of his act.

Anton listened to all the talk but did not participate beyond answering the question that one of his dinner companions posed to them all about whether anyone had seen the man? When Anton said he thought he had, there was the kind of prurient curiosity that made him uncomfortable. How had he looked? Was there anything that might have suggested? But there was nothing Anton could say to nourish the conclusions each had already reached about why a man might put a gun to his temple and fire. Nothing certain beyond sadness for his wife. Nothing beyond wild speculation and easy interpretations. Anton's wife looked surprised to hear that he had seen the man on the beach, and after the conversation turned to other things, to politics and whether Truman could secure the Democratic nomination against what seemed like a groundswell to recruit General Eisenhower to be the Democratic nominee, she asked him in a low voice why he hadn't told her. There was nothing to tell, he whispered to her. Before he did it, to anyone who saw him, he was just a guy playing with his kid on the beach.

During their exchange, the talk around the table shifted to the question of how one might craft a campaign for Truman who, they all agreed, was fairly dull and too homespun to excite anyone. "That's his slant then," one of the ad men said. "That's how to pitch him. People love that 'aw shucks' stuff." Jokes followed about all the potential candidates' assets and foibles, with some arguments about their policies. Contain the Commies? Ignore them? Insulate America from the world? Anton's wife, hugging close to him, whispered that she was bored by all the political talk. They shared a secret moment of agreement, but there was no way to politely extract themselves. The men in whose company he now sat were his peers and competitors. He needed to observe them, gauge their depth, even at the cost of

12

some social boredom. He gave his wife a pained look, his indication that he was on her side but what could he do? Then he turned back to the conversation. By the time brandy was served at nearly midnight, discussion of the man who had committed suicide and his motivation for doing it, and the meaning of it, was long past. From their ballroom banquette, none of them saw the hearse that was sent by the county coroner to take away the man's body, or the police forensics detective carry his leather satchel out to his car after he finished processing the room where the death had taken place. Nor did they see the widow, well after midnight, being whisked though the lobby and tucked into the back of a taxi for a ride to the airport for a flight home. By the time Anton and his wife returned to their room, the remarkable events of the day had all but faded from their thoughts. But despite his wife's lovely negligée and her obvious desire, Anton soon fell asleep, too logy to sustain an interest.

Anton awoke the next morning from what felt to him like a dreamless night. He studied himself in the mirror while he shaved, thinking about the way he had lathered up his children's faces when they were with him the previous weekend, and how his wife had made them wipe the shaving cream off before they came to the breakfast table. They had been contrite and then sullen, scolded for his action. In the moment, Anton had not come to their defense, in deference to his wife. Thinking about it now, he felt guilty and vowed to try to call them later, wish them well on their vacation with their mother. He had a full day, but he would find the time.

At breakfast, none of the men seemed to be dwelling on the suicide, and there was no talk of it during breaks in the seminars, or later in the afternoon either, on the links of the ocean-side golf course for which the hotel was justifiably famous. Anton and his wife played in a foursome that included Leonard and Sue Sobel, an affable couple from Montclair, New Jersey, they had befriended at the conference two years before. Leonard was in sports marketing, and was using a new driver he had brought down with him, which would be on sale in time for the Christmas season and which Leonard swore would revolutionize the game. He graciously let Anton use it; it had a great feel resting in his hands. As Anton and Leonard talked about marketing and strategies for peddling new versions of familiar products, Anton's wife and Sue Sobel talked about fashion and decorating and labor saving devices for the home, also avoiding any reference to the events of the previous day. At the tee on the four par eleventh hole, which had an exceptional view of both the hotel behind them and the ocean to the east, Anton's wife opined that it was the twin joys of perfect weather and tropical scenery, along with affectionate company, that made her want to be on a perpetual vacation. Everyone paused for a moment in a kind of reverential agreement. They stared out at the beach below them, where children running with their rafts were crashing into the waves, turning, then riding the breakers back to shore. Without adults hovering over them, they seemed remarkably wild. When Anton stepped away and set his ball on the tee, he concentrated his attention on his hands, making minute adjustments to his grip for maximum power and accuracy, determined to end the day at or under par. As he drew back to swing, from the direction of the beach he heard a child shriek, in terror or delight, he willed himself not to decide.

ATTRACTION

As Cheryl Wedlock, the attraction's Chief Operator, popped open the snaps on the white canvas panels that protect the restored Constitution Square Carousel at night, she found herself angrily juicing about local politics and civic pride. Just yesterday, at the official Memorial Day unveiling of the ride, the Mayor and various other dignitaries, none of whom had the slightest involvement in the actual process of getting the attraction restored, effusively acclaimed the results of the restoration. Speech after self-congratulatory speech praised the "grand and unified efforts" of these well-connected men whose last minute attachment to a project Cheryl had shepherded for over a dozen years, made her blood boil. She had been invited to sit on the dais for the dedication, but no one thought to ask her to say anything. In civic affairs, Cheryl learned over and over, effort counted far less than money. There was never any thought given by the man from the Mayor's event planning office to the notion that Cheryl ought to be invited to say a few words. There was no political reason to give her the recognition a speech would have accorded her, and "Time," as the advance man had reminded her, "is severely limited due to the Mayor's very tight schedule. The Mayor gave me strict orders to hold the dedication to under an hour." Cheryl, though the CEO of the Constitution Square Carousel Foundation, was not a political ally of the mayor, or one of the district representatives or councilmen, all of whom needed to be asked to speak, including the ones from rival parties. In addition, several low-level public arts managers in the current administration, which was entering its lame duck year, who were looking ahead to better jobs or insider promotions in the next administration, needed to be included. In Philadelphia, a city that had a Democratic mayor for nearly seventy years, things, if they worked right, as they were supposed to according these insiders, mostly rolled on from one regime to the next.

As the men spoke – and they were all men – some quoted, without attribution, Cheryl's booklet about the history of the Carousel. "Bringing this symbol of our artisan past to life again," she had written, "reminds us how art and industry came together in the nineteenth century." Except that the representative who used that particular quote truncated her thought and simply added after "life again" the words "will foster civic pride." Cheryl's only mention during the ceremony came during the mayor's speech, when he thanked her for her "administrative support in the long fight to get the carousel done," as if she had been a secretary sending letters to the bigwigs who were now taking the credit for having accomplished this unlikely urban miracle. Though she was gratified that the mayor thanked her for her work, he misremembered her name, calling her Cheryl Wheelock.

Much of the most elaborate cow-towing, in fact, was reserved for the corporate sponsors who came in with last-minute dollars to push things over the top, once it had become abundantly clear that it was most certainly going to happen and there was no risk in putting their brands on it. To finish funding the work on the park, the city had even sold the naming rights to various walkways and groves. There was the "Woodrow Chemical Circle" and the "Merit Bank Promenade," and "The Statewide Insurance Playground and Picnic Grove." In the weeks before the dedication, in addition to the blue historical markers cast in iron and painted with raised yellow lettering that had been planted on the groomed walkways of the newly spiffed-up park to tell the story of how this neighborhood had once been the capital

16

of American Merry-Go-Round design and manufacturing, there were also corporate logos set into the flower beds next to the paths.

But now the work was done, and after years of disappointing fund raisers and under-attended "friends of the Carousel" pot lucks, and epic resistance from the city fathers to commit money to reclaim the derelict park where the attraction now stood, one of the four squares that Philadelphia founder William Penn had laid out in his original plan for the city and the last of the four to be fully restored to public utility, kids and their families could finally enjoy it. At least there was that. It was true, as the mayor had pointed out, also paraphrasing Cheryl's writing, that craftsmen from Europe migrated to Philadelphia in the nineteenth century, when instability, economic upheaval, and violence made life in even the biggest continental cities precarious. Carvers and sign painters, window and set dressers, and men adept at mechanical engineering and whimsy created, in small manufactories that had been within sight of the park, hundreds of leaping stallions with realistically detailed saddles and long flowing tails, sea horses with white foam manes, porpoises riding on crashing waves, and elephants in fez hats standing on their hind legs. Some of these sculptures were crafted to sit in stationary positions on the moving platform, and some were bisected by brass poles and hung from articulated mechanical arms that rode up and down to mimic the experience of galloping steeds or leaping mythological creatures, while calliope music wheezed in a semi-melodic way that disturbed the air. It was from shops in the neighborhoods surrounding the park that the famous Northeastern Style carousel was exported to the world, and names like the inventor Hans Tenzel and the Fischer Toboggan Company became synonymous with the "marvel of leisure" that enthralled children beginning in 1861, when the first steam-engine was strapped to what had been a human or horse driven entertainment, and the mechanized version of the merry-go-round became a standard enticement at fairs and exhibitions around the world.

Cheryl knew all of these facts. At forty-one, she was Philadelphia's resident expert on the carousel. She had spent the last more-than-decade of her life spearheading the drive to get the derelict ride up and running and Constitution Square cleaned-up. For decades the square had been a haven for the homeless, sometimes a needle park and sometimes the main battlefield in gang turf wars, depending on the decade and how ravaging the street drug of choice was at that moment. Through it all, the boarded-up and decrepit carousel had somehow survived.

She knew that the word carousel was a corruption of either the French word *carrosel* or the Italian *carosello*, and that the original idea for the carousel dated back to jousting exercises, the "little battles" that were part of a knight's training for real combat during the crusades. She had written the historical text for the signs, researched the Tenzel animals she wanted to go 'round on her merry platform, sought and bought carcasses of old carousels with money donated to the non-profit she founded, and hired the craftsmen to restore or rebuild the damaged antiques she acquired or found in the existing shell of the ride, or to create from scratch, if necessary, replica versions of their emblematic progenitors. On each of the antique animals, often hidden from obvious view, she found the burned-in initials of the original carver. Though she researched them, she could not discover the names of any of the individual artists whose initials were secreted on the inside haunches of the horses or under the hocks of the dancing elephants. They were lost to history, their marks all that remained for posterity. In her pamphlet, in their honor, she published photographs of each set of initials, her small effort to reclaim for them some small measure of historical respect.

For the restoration, Cheryl designed and sewed the canvas tenting that formed the crown of the carousel, a pattern of blue and white stripes with gold leaf accents that seemed to be spinning at great speed when the ride was in motion, modeled on a drawing from a nineteenth century flier. She even listened to hundreds of hours of recorded calliope music to choose the songs that sounded best for what she proprietarily thought of as "her" carousel, and had them digitally cleaned up and re-mastered. Her "lucid, detailed, and profusely illustrated" history of the American carousel, and her pamphlet about the corporate history of the Fischer Toboggan Company, were both available for purchase at the Carousel ticket booth, all proceeds going back to the non-profit that ran the attraction.

As she finished stripping off the canvas overnight flaps, she stowed each one in its own compartment below the deck of the carousel, an innovation that Tenzel himself had added in the 1890's, when fairground owners complained that it took too much time to take down and fold each panel to be stowed at some other location for the day. The roustabouts who set the ride up were paid by the hour, and no one wanted them malingering over work that delayed the time at which they could crank up the steam drive on the actual ride and get paying customers aboard. Tenzel designed perfectly sized compartments that easily accommodated each canvas panel. Was it any wonder that his flying horse attractions were among the most popular in the nation?

As it was only the second day of actual operation, Cheryl felt duty bound to be present on site. She was hoping that yesterday's publicity would generate interest. There had been a picture on the front page of this morning's paper, the Inquirer, the last survivor in a once robust newspaper town, of the dignitaries standing on the dais during yesterday's ceremony, though Cheryl, at the far end, was cut off. A second, smaller shot, of the first two riders, a fifteen-year-old named Scott Wilson and his girlfriend, who only gave her first name, Sophia, appeared lower in the article. The article and pictures were also posted at the on-line version of the paper, which had a higher readership than the actual paper one. Cheryl's arm had made it into the picture with the kids, handing Scott his ticket, the only evidence of her presence. Now she waited for others to arrive, the hoped-for mothers and kids, the out of town tourists seeking the ice cream stand, the afternoon play groups, the nannies and their charges, and strolling teenagers, like Scott and Sophia, on their first sweet dates.

Cheryl had begun the process of hiring additional operators, but she wanted to test the crowds and the timing before she made any commitments, determined not to over-hire workers her non-profit could not afford. But if she was totally honest about it, beyond the proprietary feelings she had about the attraction, the fact was that she really loved operating the ride. It had been this that had motivated her from the beginning, and being the carousel driver seemed to her a perfect, if unlikely, day job for her, one to which she felt suited by temperament and inclination. She loved kids, for one thing, though wanted none herself, and was perfectly delighted to deliver them a happy, if slightly antiquated experience and then see them on their way. And far from feeling like the metaphor of the merry-go-round would come to define her professional life, she was content with the idea that she had restored this quaint vehicle to the urban landscape, a century after it first arrived, back when a growing middle class had money enough and leisure to take joy themselves in riding in circles. In fact, the resurgent leisure class of urban dwellers who had recently re-gentrified the neighborhoods around the square, repurposing the old manufactories and warehouses into lavish condos and apartments, were in many ways a parallel to their now century-gone forbearers. Like modern Americans, American Victorians fetishized their children and grandchildren, loved their free time, and saw urban parks as the stand-in for the natural world they rarely experienced.

And Cheryl had plans. Though it was not yet completed, she had found, and was having restored, a brass ring dispenser, which she planned to introduce mid-season, as soon as they were beyond the shake-down period and she could work with her mechanics on it.

The phrase "chasing the brass ring" came into the vernacular when amusement park operators saw that the inside seats – fixed, un-galloping animals and high-backed benches – were less popular with riders than the moving outside ring of animals. Rather than boarding the ride after all the outside saddles were filled, people, especially older children and teenage boys, waited for the next ride, unwilling to sit on the unmoving inside seats. This meant that the ride often circled half empty. Some manufacturers simply installed moving creatures across the whole deck, but that risked keeping women in full dresses and elderly riders off what was being aggressively billed as a "Family Attraction." Establishing a game that would be exciting to play on the fixed inside ring created a demand for those seats as well, especially when the prize for the rider who found him or herself in possession of a brass ring was a free ride. Grabbing for the brass ring proved so popular that eventually there were ring games created and installed for the moving riders as well.

It was three weeks into the summer when the first incident of vandalism occurred. Cheryl hadn't even noticed it herself; it was so minor. One of the new operators, who worked morning shift, noticed that one of the canvas panels used to protect the ride at night had been pulled down and was torn. There was no way the panel had fallen by itself – Cheryl tested the snaps that held it in place, and she herself had put it up the night before. She did not think the tear could have been made in the process of rolling it up or putting the panel away, or taking it out of its storage place beneath the deck. The tear had occurred when someone torqued the canvas the wrong way, pulling it down without knowing where the snaps were.

Cheryl executed a temporary repair on the panel using duct tape, neatly laying out the panel and carefully overlapping the sides of the torn piece a fraction of an inch, and then taping the inside along and then across the tear. She tested the fix to convince herself it would hold, at least until she was able to order a replacement, rolling it and unrolling it several times. When she was satisfied, she stowed the panel under the deck and did a careful inspection of the rest of the ride. She wondered if someone had intentionally vandalized the panel and was trying to send a message of some sort, though what the message could possibly have been, or what anger the person might harbor, or how the ride might invoke a destructive impulse she could not imagine. If it was intrusive in any way she might be able to understand it, the sound causing nearby homeowners to bristle perhaps, or crowds causing some sort of neighborhood problem like excess litter. But the park was well policed for litter by the owners of the ice cream stand, and there were no homes near enough by to hear the recorded calliope music, and while attendance had met projections there were hardly hordes of people flocking to the ride. She decided it was simply a piece of thoughtless urban nastiness, probably perpetrated by kids, and decided it was not worth any more worry. Nothing important had been damaged. The deck and the mechanicals were all untouched, and the horses and other carved animals were unmolested. After talking it over with the other operator, she decided not even to report it to the police.

Over the next three weeks, three other minor pieces of damage appeared, discovered on three successive Wednesday mornings. One night, someone spray-painted "Raygun" in white on the window of the ticket booth. She assumed it was a tag, the name of someone asserting a territorial claim to the park or to the carousel itself, during the hours when she and the riders weren't around. She trudged to the nearby hardware store and bought a paint scraper and scraped at the word herself until it was gone. A week later someone hopped the fence and unsnapped but did not damage one of the panels. Whoever it was had climbed onto the deck and left the remains of what was obviously a meal for two on one of the bench seats. There was a large pizza box, two paper plates stained with grease and tomato sauce, and a waxed paper bag, which announced in bold red lettering that its contents had been a "giant double chocolate chip cookie." There were also two half-full cans of Coors Light pushed to one corner of one of the facing benches. On the other bench, was a package that once contained a condom, though its former contents were nowhere to be found, about which Cheryl was very grateful.

Cheryl again debated whether or not to call the police, finally deciding that despite the lack of damage, she wanted to go on record about the intrusion, in case the person or people escalated or there was more damage next time, if there was a next time. When the cruiser arrived, pulling right up to the ride in the middle of the park in the middle of the day, making parents and children scatter and giving the impression that something significantly bad was going on at the moment, Cheryl left the booth to talk to the pair of officers. She showed the police partners the torn panel, and the place on the booth where the window had been spray-painted. She showed them to bench seats where she found the pizza dinner and the condom wrapper. The female officer dutifully wrote all of the information down. Her partner told Cheryl that the intruder was likely a different person than the tagger, because "the tag was an old school territory marker, but the intruders seem like kids looking for a place to have sex, which is not the same MO." And they told her that there wasn't much they could do about these events after the fact, but that they would suggest to their captain there be a few more drive-by patrols during the night.

If anything else happened, of course they should be alerted. Cheryl was satisfied that she had done her duty, thanked the officers and watched them drive away. She wondered if they would do anything, or if they were snickering behind the smoked glass of their cruiser about the crazy lady who ran the carousel.

A week later, also on a Wednesday morning, there was evidence that someone had again snuck onto the carousel in the middle of the night. This time there was no condom wrapper, but the remains of another meal, sandwiches from Subway this time, and a pair of candles, which alarmed Cheryl. The carousel was all lacquered wood, and it would go up like dried tinder if it caught on fire.

The following Tuesday, Cheryl brought her sleeping bag to work. She decided that to protect her investment in effort and time, she would see if she could catch the intruder. She felt that what he or she was doing was implicitly dangerous to the attraction, but was confident there was nothing threatening to her. When she closed the ride at eight that night, she pretended to leave, and then came back, used her key to open the gate, and slipped through one of the canvas panels onto the deck.

At about midnight, the intruders appeared. Cheryl could not see them well when they first came in. She was sitting on the deck, leaning against one of the bench seats, reading by flashlight, almost diagonally across from where they lifted the canvas panel and crawled in. She quickly doused her light and put her book down next to her. She had guessed where the intruders might come from because of where the meals had been left before, closest to their entry point, the point where a canvas panel was most shielded from view from the nearest street. She guessed that the intruder had seen the police driving by and knew how to dodge them. Now she watched through the dark as – it turned out to be *they* – lit a candle and set out their meal, pizza again, and cans Cheryl assumed were beer. She could not see them very well, but she could tell there were two of them, a man and a woman, or more likely, a boy and a girl. Cheryl listened to their conversation for a moment. Though her course of action and resolve had been clear to her a moment before, the minute they started talking she was less certain of what to do.

"Comfortable?"

"Yea." There was a pause, perhaps, Cheryl thought, for a kiss, though she could not see them clearly enough to know. Then they started to talk again, still softly, even though they did not suspect they were being overheard.

"Hungry?"

"Sure."

"It's pepperoni. From Stella's. And I have beer. Michelob Light. My brother said it was the best. Only one though. And a Diet Coke."

"Your brother never asks you about them?"

"He's not counting."

There was another moment of silence. Then she heard the pop of a can being opened, and the sound of the pizza box sliding across the bench or floor. Their silence felt tender to Cheryl, and although she was resolved to see what they were doing there, and then to show herself and shame them, her resolve had begun to disappear. When their silence went on longer than she could stand, Cheryl began to feel panic. "What if they start to have sex and I am stuck here?" she thought. Suddenly she wanted to be anywhere else than where she was, and derided herself for thinking playing detective this way was a good idea. She could not imagine why she had talked herself into doing this. Kids wanting privacy. That was the whole explanation. Thinking about her own past, her own intimate life, the furtive way early love often found its first expression, she felt suddenly shamed herself, and slid silently backwards across the deck and out under the canvas cover, leaving her book, sleeping bag, and flashlight to be retrieved later. Once outside, she resolved to stick around until they emerged, so she could gently scold them and tell them how dangerous it was to burn candles on the restored deck.

When the police car flashed its spotlight, Cheryl laughed out loud. Of course. Of course they'd catch her sneaking out of her own attraction. These officers knew nothing about the earlier intrusions, and had no idea who Cheryl was, though they quickly dropped their severe pose when she explained and showed them ID. She assured them that no one was inside, that she had just checked. The cops walked all around the ride, shining their lights into the booth and around the outside before they left.

When the kids emerged, Cheryl was waiting for them. She was surprised to see that she knew them, Sophia and her boyfriend from opening day, Scott.

"We thought you would be gone by now."

"You know you can't do this anymore. You can't come back here."

"Thanks for not ratting us out. We heard you talking to the cops. Her father would have killed her. It would have been the last straw."

"He doesn't like you two being together." They looked away; Cheryl did not need them to answer. "It's not the food, though you two are way too young to be drinking beer. It's the candle. Do you know how easily this could burn down?"

"I told him that. That's why the candle was hardly burned. I made him put it out." This endeared her to Cheryl, showed both her savvy and her sass.

"I'm really sorry." If he wasn't sincere, he did a good job of appearing to be. "We just don't have any place to go."

"I understand." Cheryl tried to seem sympathetic, remembering her own difficulties getting away from her parents. "But if I catch you here again, and I am going to be watching, I have to tell the police. You understand me? I'm serious."

"We understand." Sophia's slightly defiant tone seemed more aimed at Scott, an I-told-you-so moment of vindication for her. They hung their heads.

"Why did you tag the booth?"

"What? We didn't tag the booth. Why are you saying that?"

"Someone spray painted "Raygun" on the booth. Two weeks ago. On a Tuesday night. And why do you only come on Tuesdays?"

"It's when her father is on overnight. He's a fireman."

"Another reason why a fire here would not be a good idea. So I have to ask you, why here? Why this?"

"It was easy to get into." Scott, avoiding Cheryl's eyes, spoke flatly, simply telling her the truth. "And I like it. I like the carousel. It's like a space ship. Something from another planet. Or another time."

"Yea. The planet I live on. Geek world," Cheryl said. "Okay. Go home."

In the weeks that followed, Cheryl wondered if she should have done something to make it better, to show them things sometimes worked out for the best. Offer Scott to be an apprentice or a trainee when he got older, or found some way to honor their adult impulses.

At the end of the season, as Cheryl was washing the horses and benches to ready the ride to be mothballed for the winter, she discovered a scar on the underside brace of one of the benches. Thinking she would need to get one of the craftsmen to sand and refinish it, she got down on the deck and looked up. The scar was a small pair of initials inside a heart. The carving was neat, looking more like one of the burnt-in wood marks the craftsmen used to sign the animals when they were first made a hundred years ago than the work of an underage vandal. She wondered for a moment if she could find Scott's address or phone number, to make him come and sand and re-lacquer the damage. But running her fingers over it, she changed her mind. Let some scholar a hundred years from now puzzle over its origin, she thought. Let her wonder if it was the name of the maker of the bench. Scott had carved the initials of his name with the W of his last name expanded, to give both Sophia and him the same last name, a marriage. Nothing in Cheryl's life other than the carousel had lasted, no relationship she ever had mattered, other than this one she created with these inanimate objects. Certainly none was worth a memorial, carved or burned into anything. She was suddenly awed by Scott's audacity. She soaped up her rag and scrubbed the underside of the bench, pleased to see that the initials did not fade. They would be there as long as the attraction survived.

THE TERMINAL DANCE

Nancy wants to be a famous choreographer. Not famous, she corrects herself. Significant. Renowned. In her mind, she is eventually going to revolutionize modern dance. She wants to create choreography that recasts the conversation about movement. This is how she is working, backwards from her long-term goal to where she is now, at the start. She spends whole days thinking about where she wants to be and how to get there.

She is two years out of grad school, Master of Fine Arts, Temple University School of Dance, a solid credential but no guarantee of anything. In New York now, where she came weeks after getting her diploma, she has done a little work creating movement pieces for indie theater productions, but she has not broken out. Breaking out is the immediate goal for Nancy. She is a more than competent dancer, but she is a first-rate choreographer, her teachers have assured her. She won the departmental award for her graduate thesis. Choreography is her métier.

A group of her friends from grad school, who, like her, came up from Philadelphia to New York, have formed a company, though Nancy is the driving force behind it. Like most new arts groups, they are struggling. They don't really have a space to practice, and collectively they can afford to rent only occasionally from hourly studios. None of them has enough money to sustain a company. They all work low-wage jobs, mostly as temps.

Nancy is most often the substitute receptionist and phone answerer at a company that is a wholesale importer of fine embroidery from factories in the Czech Republic,

Slovakia, and Ukraine. The actual embroidery is done by machines, but the designs are based on traditional patterns. The silks and cottons that are the base products, tablecloths, napkins, decorative hand towels, and pillowcases, are top quality. The company repackages and resells the goods to a consortium of art museum shops, exclusive gift stores, and elite specialty and catalogue stores. She has seen the warehouse where workers fulfill orders. Her boss, Eliot Mosier, the twenty-seven-year old son of the company's founder, took her there to "show her the operation" but really to fuck her, which she guessed in advance and allowed because she was dumping her grad school boyfriend and needed to convince herself she was truly done with him. She was. She thought she had made it clear to Eliot that she was not looking for them to becoming "a thing," but Eliot continued to be interested in her. He called her in to work when she wasn't truly needed and invited her to dinner and shows. He wasn't awful, in fact he turned out to be more interesting than she had originally assumed he would be, well-read and politically liberal, and the sex had been kind of great, exciting and illicit that first time, on top of a huge pile of slippery plastic-wrapped cross-stitched tablecloths, and athletic in the midtown hotels where they went after that, but it was completely clear to Nancy that he wanted a split-level in Milburn just like his dad's, and a stay-at-home wife who took care of the kids like his mom had, and she knew she did not.

The idea that Nancy believed would start to change her profile in the dance world came to her in the Newark Airport. She was on her way to St. Croix, on a vacation she scrimped for at a cheap guesthouse she and her girlfriends once rented in college. She thought she might infuse the piece she was working on with some island-style music, Reggae and Soca, but she knew that was just an excuse for getting away from Eliot and his desire for something more permanent. And she was hoping for a quickie island romance.

Because of the PATH train schedule, she arrived at the airport at 6:25 in the morning, an hour earlier than she needed to be there. She cleared security and got to her departure gate before the American Airlines personnel even opened the kiosk. Facing the terminal, slumped in a seat near the window, she was startled out of her early morning lethargy when she noticed people parting around a slow moving janitor in a kind of parabola, their speed of movement a contrast of determination to languor, of progress to indolence, travelers heading toward their destinations and a laborer stuck in the routines of boring work; the terminal dance.

Once she had the inspiration, she worked for more than a year to refine it. She got permission from the airport authority and the TSA to return five times. Some of the conversations had been awkward.

"What are you going to be doing in the airport?" the TSA supervisor asked her suspiciously, not comprehending the language Nancy was using.

"A movement piece, based on the activity in an airport terminal."

"A dance piece?"

"Well, I prefer the word movement to dance, but yes. You can call it that."

"What will you be doing in the airport?"

"Just watching people," she told the woman. "For verisimilitude. So I get it right. My idea involves turning observable motion into choreography and building a program out of that."

"Why do you want to come back so many times? Once you see it, isn't that it? I'm in the terminal all the time. It all looks pretty much the same to me every time."

After Nancy described how she had gotten the idea for the project, the TSA supervisor said, "I have two daughters. My older girl has been taking ballet at a studio in New Brunswick for four years."

"I started in a little studio in Towson where I grew up, and I never wanted to do anything else," Nancy lied to her enthusiastically. In fact, her commitment to dance as an avocation had come late, well into her junior year at college, when a particularly inspiring instructor had praised her work in a class she took as a lark. She had danced as a kid, but had given it up after her sophomore year in high school when it started to seem uncool. She and the TSA supervisor talked about the kind of dreams parents of girls who dance have.

"Right now she covets a part in the local production of *The Nutcracker*. She's worn out one DVD of *Black Swan* already."

"I was exactly the same way. Obsessed." Nancy was pleased with herself for being able to persuade the TSA supervisor, and eventually the airport authority, and the American Airline personnel who controlled the terminal she wanted to stake out, to let her spend time just hanging around the airport. They gave her a letter and a temporary badge, and a method for checking in and clearing security. Her research method involved finding an active gate and hunkering down. She brought a large carry-on style bag with her, which held her computer, and spent the day watching how people moved through the terminal space. She stood in line for airport food, and she drank far too much airport coffee.

Over the course of a year, she observed eleven distinct kinds of movements, with multiple variations. She tracked them using a kind of flow chart she created using the sticky notes app in Scrivener. She had the idea of starting with specific movements as solos, and then filling the stage with the ensemble performing variously as workers, travelers, pilots, flight crews, airport staff, business people, vacationers, and families, all the types she observed moving through the terminal space toward departure gates, or flowing from them upon arrival. She catalogued the differences between the way people moved heading toward departure and how they moved heading toward the exit doors and baggage claim and the taxi or ground transportation stands after they arrived.

Each movement would require a different physical carriage, a different sense of urgency. She didn't want to tell any actual stories, but the movements needed to be analogical about the burdens and pleasures of travel for work, or the joys of anticipating impending leisure, or the necessity of traveling for reasons other than work or pleasure, to family reunions or bridal showers or visitations with long lost lovers, or rushing to see the diseased or dying. She watched the ways people's faces communicated or masked their feelings of longing or loss, and she guessed about the specific causes of agitation or tension. She made notes about characters, not because she wanted to create characters but because imagining their stories was a useful step toward capturing something essential about their movement, the essence of it. She knew it was inevitable that her dancers would be read as characters to some extent, especially if she costumed them at all, but she aspired to something more allegorical. She made some costume sketches, making notes about the actual clothes travelers wore, though she hoped to dress her dancers only minimally, accessorizing them with touches that suggested roles and class and styles. Although there was some appeal to the idea of making their clothes speak to their roles as Agnes de Mille did with her dancers in *Rodeo*, a seminal ballet that Nancy loved, her intention was to suggest something more abstractly universal.

On stage she thought her piece should be structured around the rhythm of the day and the increase of human traffic as the offstage flights became more frequent, from first thing in the morning, to midafternoon, to when the arrivals and departures peaked midday, and then decreasing as time descended into afternoon and night. She wanted to bookend the dance with workers, terminal cleaning personnel, with carpet sweepers and vacuum cleaners, the first-in-last-out solos of those who prepare and maintain the terminal for everyone else. She wanted to include movement that showed the way people consumed goods in airports, how food was mostly consumed pre boarding. She observed that no one arrived at the airport and stopped for a meal unless they were on a layover, and no one shopped on arrival either, unless they needed a gift for a loved one they had neglected to buy before returning to their point of origin. She observed the way people dealt with their belongings, bags and suitcases, carry-ons, and roll-aboards. She absorbed airport lingo from gate crews and baggage handlers she talked to on their breaks and in their work areas.

She hadn't gotten on her flight to the Caribbean the day she had the idea for the piece. She changed her ticket for the next day and sat in the terminal writing, drawing, making costume notes, and surreptitiously recording people and sounds on her iPhone. She'd been stuck in airports before, but so disgruntled she never paid attention to the amount of drama that swirled around her, the amount of purposeful and nervous movement. Eight million people flew every day world-wide, and how many paid attention to anything but the necessities of their own objectives, to boarding or deplaning or exiting the terminal? Now she heard the sounds of the airport as little concertos, and the sights as little movies the sounds underscored. The soundscape for her piece as she imagined it consisted entirely of specific sounds she heard at the airport, or altered or processed versions of them. PA announcements, passenger conversations, vending machine deliveries, bells used as horns on electric carts, discussions and arguments between passengers, or between passengers and gate agents, cleaning sounds, trash cans being emptied by janitors, sounds of jet way doors opening and closing, bringing in sounds of the plane engines from the tarmac, sounds of people talking on their phones on arrival, alerting loved ones they would soon emerge with their bags for pick-up, swelling into a crescendo of voices and then receding to near silence as the plane emptied and its human cargo moved off down the corridors, the swift and the slow, the healthy and the lame, safely landed after their liberation from gravity.

To create the soundscape for her piece, Nancy enlisted the brother of one of her grad school friends to build the track. He had a great facility with Pro Tools, and despite never having done anything quite like it before, the score he produced was exactly what she imagined, dense and strange and rhythmic and layered.

Before rehearsals started, she auditioned for dancers she thought her company was missing, with thoughts of both her future company and her present piece. She started to talk to publicists and eventually hired one whose job it was to convince the major newspapers and websites to include her in listings, and eventually to write reviews.

The dancers she invited to join her company were all beautiful, fit, and skilled. They represented a wide array of body types and several ethnicities. It was important to the piece that her company be as diverse as the actuality she had observed in the airport. She chose dancers so that each could perform multiple roles, workers and travelers. But she also chose people she liked. She wanted to start to build something she knew required a commitment, and so she interviewed everyone she auditioned extensively about their ideas about dance and their desires as performers, and their vision for the future of their art. She introduced her own ideas into these conversations as well, to gauge the commitment to building a company with her. She rejected dancers who did not seem able to answer her questions or articulate their ideas about where dance was headed or what it might need. She didn't care if they didn't agree with everything she said. In fact, she liked the ones who disputed her ideas the best. She rejected dancers who seemed only like they wanted to be directed rather than injecting their own ideas into the process. She wanted partners in the creative process.

During the year she worked on the piece, she continued to temp for Eliot's company, and to sleep with him. She did her best to hold him at arm's length when it came to any discussion about a future for their relationship. He seemed to understand that she was focusing on her work, and was not prepared to make any kind of immediate commitment to him, but he was persistent nevertheless.

"You have fun when you're with me, don't you?"

"I do," she had to admit to him. "I'm just not ready to commit to anything long term with anyone. I told you from the beginning. You're so old fashioned about this. It's a hook-up world out there. That's the world I run in. My friends already think I'm nuts for spending as much time with you as I do."

Nancy never said explicitly that she and Eliot were exclusive sexually, and he did not ask, but she knew he believed they were. During her work on her terminal project she developed an attraction to one of her dancers, and had recently started sleeping with him as well. She assumed that if Eliot knew about it, he would break things off with her. And she thought about telling him so that would happen. But she didn't want to feel that she was choosing one over the other, or that one mattered over the other in that way. It wasn't Eliot's business who she slept with, or what else was in her *private* life. Nor did she feel that it was necessary to tell the dancer what she was doing with Eliot. It was irrelevant to them.

The dancer was named Peter Clark. In addition to being a superb performer, he had great ideas and had quickly become her sounding board as she honed her ideas into a coherent evening of suites. In some ways, she felt that once they had started to talk about her work it was inevitable that they would become lovers. There were others in the company whose contributions mattered to her, and she listened intently in rehearsals to all of her dancers' ideas. She told them at the first rehearsal that she would, and that "one never knew where a great idea would come from." But it was Peter, increasingly, she relied on to respond to her ideas.

Rehearsals went well, though they were hampered by limited funds. She wanted more time to work things out, but convinced herself that all performing artists feel that way as opening night approaches. "If only we had another week of rehearsal," she had heard her theater friends say, sometimes authentically critiquing their under-rehearsed openings, sometimes deflecting their pride in what they had actually accomplished. In the case of Nancy's company she resigned herself to what she had, and to being ready when opening came. But two weeks before they were scheduled to begin with a preview show, it became clear to her that despite the best efforts of her publicists, and the hard work of her company members soliciting ticket sales through their web site and from their friends, and a fairly well produced video and Indiegogo campaign, advanced ticket sales were lackluster and they would not make their fundraising goal, perhaps not even have enough to pay the final installment for the theater space when it was due the week before opening.

Artistically, she felt like she and her company were creating something terrific, and if it was less ground-breaking than she thought it might be, it was clearly the calling card of a serious young artist, a step on the way to her long-term goal. She desperately wanted a *Times* review, an extended notice in *Time Out* and in *The New Yorker*, and consideration in *danceviewtimes*, as well as coverage in the smaller weeklies that drove ticket sales.

She concealed her worries from her company and from Eliot, though she talked about them at length with Peter.

"What if no one comes?"

"You already have ticket sales for every night of your run. People are coming."

"Not enough. And what if the media doesn't come? I know some people will blog and I'll get some chop from my Twitter followers and on Instagram. But is that going to be enough?"

"Enough for what? If the work is great, who cares? And you know I think the work is great."

Nancy hated conversations like this when they took place in bed. She was naked, and she and Peter had just finished making love. She felt that she could not completely trust anything he said after sex, influenced, as it was, by their physical connection and the complex logic of being together. She did not trust that there was not an element of flattery in his responses to her, or gamesmanship, though she knew that it was more likely that Eliot would respond to her that way than Peter. Still, her experience with men told her that there was a hint of dishonesty in every post-coital conversation, especially if the sex was good and there was an implied desire to repeat it at some time in the future.

"I know I should be thinking of the work alone, but I can't. It's not how I'm wired. It has to matter. It has to become part of the conversation."

"Matter to whom? It will be lovely and true or it won't. That's all that matters. Isn't that what you've been saying in rehearsals for weeks now?"

What Nancy could not say to him directly, of course, was how much it mattered to her that *she* matter, that *she* be part of the conversation, by which she meant the conversation within the larger artistic community, by which she meant that she would be talked about in the world beyond herself.

"Why do it if there is no impact? If no one says, 'That was new,' or 'That will change things,' or even, 'That's the best thing I have seen in a long time?'"

At a loss for how to respond to this in any useful way, Peter stroked her back. But she was beyond being gentled out of her reverie. She got out of bed and pulled on her tee shirt and jeans. She went to her kitchen and sat at the table, looking out at the corner of Manhattan she could see from her apartment. When she went back into the bedroom fifteen minutes later, Peter was asleep.

The week before opening, she was twenty-three hundred dollars short of what she needed to pay the last installment on the theater, not to mention what she needed to pay her dancers and crew. "How did I let myself be such a Pollyanna about this?" she asked aloud, sitting in her kitchen looking at the advance ticket sales reports on line. She had a fair certainty that the reviewers would come – there had been a bit of a buzz created by her publicist, in part because she had let some of the smaller papers send photographers to rehearsals rather than just providing them with publicity stills. But she despaired that there would be a last minute surge of ticket sales. Everything about the program felt right to her, ready, but now, here on the cusp of seeing it performed, of testing her vision and her artistry with the public and her peers, it seemed possible that it would collapse.

She called Eliot. "I need you to lend me forty-five hundred dollars," she told him. "I'm short money I need to pay rent on the theater space and to pay my dancers. I'll pay you back, however long it takes. Is there any way?"

The performance went off, not without a hitch but with no visible blunders that would have been fatal to the artistry of the piece. In fact, though the *Times* did not send anyone on opening night, most of the other reviewers came, and there were positive notices in most of their columns and blogs, and objective descriptions her publicist had written in the listings sections of the rest. The *Times* came on the third night, and as a result of the reviews an increased audience arrived in the second week (there were three shows each of the two weeks) and ticket sales enabled Nancy to breathe easier that she would be able to pay back Eliot's loan. More than a few of her peers in the dance community came to see her shows, and at the opening party and on the street afterward, people she respected from the community, other dancers and choreographers, talked to her about what they saw, all in generally positive if not glowing terms. The exception turned out to be *The Times*, whose reviewer said that Nancy's work, "while competent and clever, did not break new ground either as a cohesive proposal for a revived approach to thematic dance or as a kind of radical, non-verbal movement theater," referring, in both cases, to things she had said in the "Choreographer's Notes" she had written in the program. While the rest of the review praised the precision of the company, singling out several of the individual dancers for praise, most particularly Peter, and remarking on "the elegance of the opening and closing movements, which evoked the wistful desire to get away among people who, because of their menial jobs, are close to the gates of flight but cannot ever take it," Nancy felt slighted by it. The review came out after the first week, during which the audience was largely made up people who had first or second-hand contact with her or members of the company. Ticket sales for the shows during the second week were better overall, but slower than she wanted, and she took the *Times* review and the resulting decent but not-sold-out houses as a verdict about her work, and was disappointed that her year-long effort had not more dramatically advanced her career toward its goal. In fact, in deriding her choreography while praising the work of her dancers, it almost seemed to Nancy that the *Times* reviewer was suggesting that they had contributed the more inventive and important part of the piece.

After the fact, she evaluated for herself what it had meant to work with each of the dancers. She considered who she wanted to continue to work with and who had not fulfilled her expectations. Eliot offered to help her set up a business structure that would lead to non-profit status so she could raise funds for future projects and put her company on a better footing. Though he knew she did not feel she had arrived at her goal, he assured her that despite the *Times*, she was launched. She had made a statement with a new company and if the outcome was not as significant artistically as what she was hoping for, neither was the result "the disaster you feared it might be when you asked me for that loan."

He pointed out that *The New Yorker* had called the work "smart, esoteric, and inviting," and that *danceviewtimes* had said that it "demonstrated that a scrappy new company can still bring fresh and enticing work to the New York dance scene." Despite his best efforts, she could not give in to his comforting her.

Weeks after the last performance Nancy was still scuffling for work. She had naively hoped, maybe even expected, that word of mouth in the dance and theater communities would bring her more attention, and more high-level work, but it had not happened. In the months that followed the performance, she did not receive a single call that suggested work was forthcoming as a result of her company's performance. She was impatient to move on from temping, to shift from living the life of a part-time artist and full-time wage-earner to living a more balanced artistic existence. In her best moments, she knew that she was on the right track. In her worst, she could not stand how little seemed to have changed, or how the *Times* review had made her feel diminished.

She continued to see both Eliot and Peter, without making a commitment to either, which was fine with Peter but frustrating to Eliot, on whom the performance he supported with his generosity had a dramatic impact.

"Let me be your patron," he told her. "Let me support you. I have plenty of money. I love what you did. I want to help you keep doing it. We would make a great team. You have a great talent, and it would make me very happy to help sustain it." But she did not trust his appraisal;

in fact, felt it more self-serving than supportive. Eliot, she concluded, liked being the source of money for her artistic endeavors, liked having her dependent on him. Not that he didn't want to be with her, or even, she shuddered slightly to consider, love her. But he was blind to the meaning of his support for her, to the way it made her feel, to the way it diminished her independence. She resisted his offer, continuing to sleep with him and work for him intermittently, until six months later he told her that he would not hire her any more.

"I can't do this. It feels wrong to keep employing you when what I really want is to live with you, to be part of your life in another way altogether."

The following Monday she registered with another temp agency and within a week she was working as the receptionist for an elite private school in Midtown.

She told Peter about the change. By then he knew all about her relationship with Eliot. He had disapproved, not at all because she had been sleeping with Eliot at the same time she had been sleeping with him, but because he thought taking Eliot's money had been the easy way out.

"You want to know my opinion?" he asked her.

"Sure," she told him, though she was not sure.

"When you breathed out, when you sighed in relief that that show would go on after you asked him for his dough, and he said he would give it to you, things got a little softer. There was something better about the work when you were wound up like a top."

"That's not fair. The two things were completely separate."

"That is not how I saw it. The minute the risk of disaster dropped out of it, you got soft on everyone. The last two rehearsals were love fests. You should have been cracking the whip."

"The last two rehearsals? Things were in great shape by then."

"Yes. But they could have ratcheted up. You let everyone relax by showing them you were relaxed."

"What should I have done? We couldn't have paid our rent."

"You beg the landlord. You blow him if you need to. I don't know. You don't give in to easy. Nothing great has ever come by giving in to easy."

"I can't believe you are telling me this now." They were in bed. She was naked. It occurred to her that this was when Peter liked to start important conversation, and as much as she distrusted his praise, she distrusted his critique.

"This is jealousy. You're having a little revenge because I was fucking him at the same time I was fucking you. You come on all open minded but you're as possessive as he is."

"That's bullshit and you know it. I'm telling you a truth about yourself. You want something you are not willing to really put yourself on the line to have."

Nancy spun out of bed and retreated to her kitchen. Hadn't she put herself on the line for the piece by creating it? With all the work she did to bring it to stage? Wasn't that enough? To her back Peter said, "You were whoring yourself out to a sugar daddy you knew would come in handy one day. And he paid off."

After Peter had gotten dressed and left her apartment, she tried to reconstruct the argument, to see if it had any validity or if it had arisen out of some particle of sexual jealousy she had not previously understood. She wondered if Peter had intended to break up with her and had chosen this way to do it, or if she could have seen this coming. She even wondered if breaking up with Eliot had caused Peter to panic, to feel that she might be consolidating her relationship with him into something exclusive or singular. But try as she might, she could not untangle her anger from her hurt, and for a long time after, as angry as she was, and sure that she had talent and vision as she was, nothing she did produced the certainty that she was on to an idea as rich as the one she had months before, working on her terminal dance.

BURDEN OF SECRETS

On her way to the post office, Ellen Taylor wondered, not for the first time, how much of the pleasure of getting letters from Richard came from the fact that they existed as physical objects. She could handle them, count them, sort them by date, by place of composition, by primary subject, by length. She could feel each one's specific weight, heft each one in her hands. Richard's letters were her only true secret, living a life that was, like most people's these days, frantically public. Like her friends and family, her work and social life was arranged in the relatively exposed world of shared Outlook calendars, on breezy Facebook posts, or networking via LinkedIn. Details were worked out in emails or in IM's, fast, electronic, and supposedly ephemeral, but she knew from watching police procedurals on TV and reading about personal exposure in lurid court cases, that these supposedly instant blips of information left permanent and telltale tracks. Discoveries happened. A husband innocently logs on to his wife's machine looking for an email address and discovers a lover's naked picture in a supposedly secure folder. A child plays a game on his father's laptop and discovers a cache of porn. An email is inadvertently sent to an entire mailing list when it was meant for a single person. Common accidents, disastrous exposures. She cringed at the way some of her friends and younger colleagues told all their secrets on line, used blogs or Facebook to expose details of their daily lives she herself neither wanted to expose nor, frankly, read about, though she did sometimes voyeur her friends' confessions, obsessively, if guiltily. Though fully conversant in the operation and

45

capabilities of computers, fundamentally she distrusted them, and believed that even impersonal technology could prove to be a very personal betrayer. A real letter on the other hand, written on standard lined paper, tri-folded and sent in a number ten envelope, read, then filed in a manila rather than a virtual folder, and stored not on a drive but in a drawer, somehow felt to Ellen, despite the long history of exposure of characters through letters in literature, less likely, these days, ever to become public property. Letters had become, somehow, the safer, more anonymous alternative.

She was playing *The Band* on the car stereo, a song she had been listening to for years, "Long Black Veil," about a man wrongly accused of murder who goes to his death rather than reveal his alibi – that he had been in the arms of his best friend's wife. The song's chorus was among Ellen's favorites, "Nobody knows and nobody sees. Nobody knows but me." In the Band's version, the "me" was drawn out to the point where it was almost comical, a wailing vocal reveal of what is supposed to be a shameful secret.

At the post office she went to her box. The clerks all knew her and waved as she walked through the lobby. She wondered, without really caring, if they guessed why she maintained the box. She checked her box once or twice a week. Most often it was empty. For nearly thirty years she had been receiving letters three or four times a year from the man with whom she had a brief love affair just out of college, but whose impact on and presence in her life had continued through all of her marriage to Paul, through having and raising Ray, through graduate school, through her career success, through everything. For years the letters arrived at random intervals, not birthdays or holidays but, she had come to understand, when she was on his mind, when it meant something to him to write to her.

Ellen had recently debated, while narrating to her latest therapist the current ups and downs – mostly downs – of her marriage to Paul, whether or not to confess her ongoing relationship via correspondence with Richard. Therapists had warned her over the years that as long as she idealized an absent lover she would never be able to fully commit to a relationship with an actual, present one. But she failed to see how one even impacted the other. Her entire relationship with Richard for over thirty years had been literary. Or at least his letters to her had been literary. She knew that he appreciated her responses, filled with news and facts about her work, her family, her everyday life. But Richard was a writer and unlike her letters to him, his letters were dense with something other than events. They were filled with his peculiar, attenuated love for her, she supposed she would say if anyone ever asked her to characterize it, but also more than that. His letters to her were particular, surprising, poetic, written to be savored and then saved and cherished. His letters, what she had come to think of as "the letters," were expressive of his singular state of mind at the time of their composition. They were a diary of his enigmatic heart, an astonishing chronicle of interest in the natural and human world, from the perspective of someone who dwelt just slightly askew from both. Hers, she knew, compared to his, were mundane. Generic. She cringed at the word, but it was accurate. His letters were not written in the relaxed prose of familiar exchange between old friends. They were fraught, by turns pained and ecstatic. She wondered, sometimes, if the intensity with which he lived his life was a kind of madness, as she wondered at times if her rather work-a-day letters to him – the letters of a decent but uninspired correspondent – held anything more than casual interest for him, if they disappointed him in some way, though she had never had any indication of that. It was in person that she was able to best express what she felt for him, in talk and with sex particularly, though it had been years since they had been to bed together or really had any extended time together for relaxed, unfolding conversation. Whether he anticipated her letters to him, or craved them at all the way she did his, she did not know. She did not know if they were satisfying, the way his always felt to her, like a meal rather than a snack, like a full night's sleep and not a half-hour sprawl-down on the couch. Despite their lack of face-to-face contact, his letters remained the same, intimate-feeling and powerful, the letters of a lover. Hers, she worried, despite her desire that they be more, contain more, express more, were predictable, obvious, chatty letters from, well, a friend.

The arrival of his letters defined when they connected, what they shared. She never sent letters to him except in response to his letters to her. There had never been discussion of this; it was simply how the correspondence had evolved. He was the writer; he wrote to her. She was his audience, perhaps, she allowed herself to believe, his occasional muse. Her letters were applause; his letters were performance. But it was the fact that they were each other's secret that had, as much as anything, convinced her at the last moment not to tell the therapist about their ongoing connection. Revealing that there was a history, she thought, and saying something about how powerfully that history still influenced her, held dangers. She had not seen the therapist long enough to feel sure that she could be trusted not to simply stall at the revelation, to insist what the other therapists had insisted: that she would never be fully invested in her marriage until she put aside her clearly illicit if non-sexual relationship with Richard. Ellen had come to see this response as a drastic over-simplification. Investment in her relationship with Paul had never been an issue for her. There was no quotidian reality to her relationship with Richard. If there had been no investment in her relationship with Paul there would be no pain in it. And there was pain. There was no possibility that she would run off with Richard. He had never asked, and she was sure he never would. It had been her decision, long ago, to opt for the things Richard was not offering, family, stability, daily companionship, love of a

48

formal if unevenly passionate variety. Not to mention a home, steady work, health care, and stuff. Ellen liked stuff, clothes, books, *objets d'art*, too much to give them up. Nor was Ellen certain that she could articulate to the therapist why she protected her correspondence from the possibility of discovery with the relatively elaborate ruse, for her, of a postal box, of an intentionally mislabeled file in her office filing cabinet, when, even if it had been discovered, there would be no likely consequence. Paul knew all of the details of her face-to-face relationship with Richard, the part that occurred years ago, because he had been witness to all of it. She did not know if Paul would be jealous or angry with her for this tenuous continuation of it. She simply didn't want him to be part of it. Or a therapist with a shallow understanding of it to make dramatic conclusions about it.

The box, to her surprise, had two items in it. Although no one else knew about the box and therefore she should have received no other mail there, she occasionally got junk addressed to "Box Holder." She hated when that happened. There was a little window in the front of the box so she could see if there was anything inside before she opened the door. When the box contained mail, she had an involuntary pang of joyous anticipation as she fumbled to fit the oddly shaped key into the lock, only to be disappointed by some offer to sign up for supplemental health insurance or get her storm windows replaced.

Her habit was to check the postmarks first. These two were both from out west, not surprising, as Richard had not been east of Colorado for years, one from Missoula and the other, a post card, from what looked like Billings. The stamp on the back was canceled with a smear that crossed the card and made the mailing P.O. impossible to read. The post card was a glossy shot of a western small town street, totally unimpressive, with the note "thinking of you" written on it in pencil, and signed "Love." No name. They had long ago given up signing their letters, another hedge against discovery. It was stupid, of course, because discovery would have meant revelation with or without the signatures, but it was ritual now. If anyone wanted to make an issue out of her correspondence with Richard, the lack of signatures would hardly have given her any deniability.

Richard had no attachments. No family, dead parents, no siblings. There would be no consequence for him if their letters came to light that she could imagine, so the subterfuge was all for her. She assumed that he kept all of her letters, but, of course, he might simply read her letters and toss them out, travelling light as he did, but she did not want to think about that. She wanted to believe in their existence, the separated sides of a torn dollar, the way the long lost would prove their connection one day in the future.

The second item in the box was a letter. Mailed in a cheap safety envelope, it had some heft to it, and she decided to take it to Starbucks to read it rather than stand in the P.O. She liked Starbucks because she knew she was invisible there. Starbucks was completely generic, a McDonald's for coffee lovers. Years ago, in the late 1980's, she had had coffee in the original Starbucks at Pike Place Market in Seattle. It was just before they went national and there was the coffee-shop explosion, and it seemed a glorious idea – a temple to coffee – and she recognized her response as the tingle of a junkie who had just discovered the perfect new source for her fix. Nearly thirty years later, the nation was awash in dark roast, and she was simply another caffeine addict on the way to work. There were six Starbucks within a five-block radius of her office, but her favorite one was in the lobby of the Bellevue Hotel, about half way between the post office and her office. The shop was part of what had once been a vaulted lobby entrance, the part of the entrance where a liveried doorman would have waited to bring out an umbrella to a guest emerging from a taxi in the rain, or where the luggage carts might have once been stored. Now a drive-up entrance had been created on the side of the hotel and this space had been repurposed. The baristas who worked there in the morning – and had for years – never even looked at her. They did their work, did not relate to customers. She assumed they were sisters, they looked that much alike, but perhaps they were simply aping each other's styles. They were both slightly overweight, but, in the style of the moment, wore their hair and clothes in a way that emphasized their sensuality, Lycra blouses tight around the midriff and low cut, form fitting pants, clothes that showed skin in a casual way, never quite covering exposed bellies or backs. This was distinctly different from the prevailing style of her late twenties, when legions of women invading formerly all-male professions had dressed their sexuality down by dressing up in business suits and angular masculinized jackets. Being soft and sexy disqualified you from being taken seriously in those days, and her desire to succeed in her profession had seemed worth the sacrifice then. Now she wondered if she had not given up something important. Looking at these women, Ellen recognized that even the attempts to corral them into server uniforms was being subverted by the very way they wore them; their Starbucks aprons were somehow off, tied low, slung or slid off to the side. They were like the slightly slutty parochial school girls from her childhood who managed to wear their dull uniforms in ways that undermined the very intent of uniformity, making them totally alluring to boys, shocking to good girls like her, and the bane of parents' and teachers' existences. The baristas had nearly matching lip rings, and each wore her hair piled rather than styled on her head. Both women had tattoos, and over time Ellen had noticed new ones being inked on to their arms and legs. But they seemed to have a sense of humor about themselves, and teased each other about how they looked. Ellen had heard their banter. They might have even been lovers, though their talk never seemed flirty as it did friendly. But who knew anymore? People did what they did, hid their private lives in public.

She was doing it, though clutching the letter seemed so quaint to her that thinking about it made her laugh. Who sent letters anymore? No one.

The letter, when she was settled into an armchair with a latte and coffee cake, was what she had come to expect from Richard – funny, specific, and deeply personal, but lacking details of the most basic kind about the location or circumstance of its composition. Her letters routinely started with such information. "I am sitting in the Starbucks near work. The weather is brutal today, hot and humid...." She had come to see the absence of these niceties as proof that he was really thinking specifically of her, not just writing a generic here's-how-I-am letter. This letter was decorated with a picture of an amethyst cut from an advertising catalog or newspaper insert. Amethyst was her birthstone. It occurred to Ellen that no one she wrote emails to on a regular basis retained any of the creativity that letters to and from her friends had once been full of – puzzle letters and collages and letters with cartoons and drawings. When had those letters stopped coming regularly? When had she stopped writing them? Richard continued to make the act of opening a letter something more than the necessary precursor to reading it.

"Dear Heart," this letter began, one of a number of Richard's thirty-plus-year running jokes. His letters were anything but conventional sentimental love letters, but the fluttery language of love letters intrigued him. He liked that for all its repetition there was no other kind of correspondence that would begin with words like "dear heart." Terms of endearment were perhaps once tossed off with a casualness that made the susceptible fall for each other more eagerly. In the normal world, had these words been used in earnest they would be suspect. But in Richard's logic, or perversity, using them made them substantial, meaningful. It occurred to her that Richard's use of decorative language and his somewhat overblown style was romantic in part because he was so out of touch with the world.

He was probably the brightest man she had ever known well, a mind so naturally agile it was often dazzling. Yet from long before she had met him, Richard had decided that there was nothing really worth doing in life except seeing where it would take him. He thought of himself as a professional observer. He lived free and poor, with an almost Zen-like absence of ambition, and managed to get by on stretches of low-level work between long periods of travel, short stints of couch-surfing, camping, and beach-bumming. When she met him, at the school for disabled kids where they both worked for a while after college, he was in the middle of what would turn out to be the longest job he ever held, over eighteen months. He had as anarchistic a life as one could have and still be in control of it. He was the only person she knew who had managed to sit out the Reagan, Bush, Clinton, and Bush years, unimpressed with the well-hyped yuppie version of how to get ahead and live the good life. He had what he needed, he told her. A duffle bag of clothes. Library cards. A tent and sleeping bag if needed. For periods of time, a car he lived out of. A Coleman stove. A small rotating number of used books he traded for other books at secondhand stores and Goodwill. Maps of state parks with campgrounds. A dozen or so post office boxes across the plains and mountain states and up into the far west. He had once quoted her a line from a Charles Olson poem she still remembered: "In a time of plenty, go side, go smashing...."

A couple of times a year he sent her an itinerary, very rough and not reliable, but to be used as a guide for where to send her next letter. Sometimes she missed by days his coming or going, meaning it might be months or even years before he returned to that P.O. and retrieved her letter, removing any sense of its urgency or moment, which, she recognized, made her attempts to ground her letters with specific information about weather or location particularly absurd. He lived, in short, a kind of life thought to be impossible in America, one blissfully unattached to merchandise, to acquisition, to the work-to-get-ahead ethic, to anything that resembled stable middle-classism. He was a wanderer, a man in the tradition of the early troubadours, a man without roots, without boundaries, without destination.

Once in a while she still thought of running away with him, of what it would be like to live with him the way he lived, without fixed address, without permanent work, without, she knew, the possibility of having a specific day-to-day impact on the world. Was it merely self-flattery that her work was important enough to be taken by her as essential? Was she doing anything that anyone as well trained or experienced as she couldn't do? These thoughts deviled her. But she had long ago convinced herself that she would never be happy and it would never work, that his was a life which could only be lived solo, and that she would only tolerate it for so long before she would crave home, family, hot shower, and a mattress that conformed to her body. These days, the only time it came up was when she was really angry at Paul and she fantasized about just chucking it all and running away. She knew it was out of the question to ask Richard to give up his choices and settle down with or for her.

His actual life style was not without some appeal. Other than his clothes and personal items, he really owned nothing and therefore had responsibility for nothing. He did seasonal work if he worked at all. Most years he worked as a department store Santa from November to December, a job that paid surprisingly well. In his younger days he had had to wear an artificial belly, wig, and beard. Now the beard and hair at least were real and snow white. The hair he wore in a ponytail in all of his very occasional recent pictures – it was never clear who had taken them – had become the flowing locks of an authentic Santa. He was great with kids, and parents loved him, or so he reported. He told her that his Christmas job made him genuinely jolly. She concluded this must be true since he had been working the same mall in

Seattle for two decades. He was also their Easter Bunny, and the odd Disney or Pixar character during special promotions if he was in town. Recently there was a week when malls across the country gave away free books and used Dr. Seuss's *The Cat in the Hat* as their charity shill. He sent her a picture of himself in costume from a local paper shaking hands with some official. He wrote her that the Cat had always been his favorite character. A few summers back he had done a stint as Nemo's father, the Clownfish, that amused him a great deal. He had charm, and enough skill as an actor that he could make people – kids at least – believe in his happiness. His ennui, for there was always also that, he rendered invisible.

Between these jobs he wandered the country. He wrote, sometimes professionally for travel journals, sometimes short articles for business travel websites, sometimes book reviews. He did occasional pieces about obscure places and kitsch museums. It had gotten easier to make a minor living as this kind of writer since the inception of the Internet because he didn't need to be anywhere specific to correspond with editors. He had a manila envelope filled with library cards from hundreds of towns, places where he could use the Internet for free. Of course, she had never seen the envelope, or anything else that he carried with him. He was, for all intents and purposes, a fictional character himself, a writer's invention. She could no more verify that he did what he said than she could verify that there was a molten core to the earth. But she believed fervently in his accounts. She did not believe he was capable of lying.

For years she worried about him. He seemed to her, at times, to live on nothing. *"Luftmensch,"* she had once heard one of her Jewish friends call his type, men who lived on air. He had no insurance and she worried that his peripatetic life would one day weaken him, infect him, kill him. Or that an injury would kill him. When she wrote to him once about these fears he wrote back that he was in no more danger of dying than she, that he had a fair amount of comfort if rarely a lot of space, and that he knew enough to stay out of the rain.

He rented a room if he found himself in a weather-bitten city. For a period of time in the 1990's he had owned a used panel van, fitted out with a bed, an eating area, an ersatz kitchen with a propane stove and dry sink, and a tiny pantry. He had lived along the east coast during this period of time – in Vermont during the summer and in Jacksonville in the winter – and she had actually seen him once, passing through Philadelphia, though he would not show her the van – wouldn't "take her home" as he had put it. She had been relieved. She was afraid that she would have climbed into its foam rubber platform bed with him and never gotten out. Instead, they met in a diner. He told her how he orchestrated his life, joining fitness clubs or Y's that had daily or weekly or monthly memberships, which gave him access to showers and bathrooms. He regularly used libraries and college facilities when he needed to during the day. And he spent his time exploring, working temp jobs when he needed to, reading, going to museums, and doing his laundry. He told her that if he was showered and groomed, if his clothes were washed and in good repair, if his hair was neat and combed – even long – no one took him for homeless. If his lack of address came up with his employers – it rarely did for temporary workers – his ready explanation that he had just moved to town and was staying with friends usually sufficed. He had friends around the country, and he sometimes used their addresses if his P.O. boxes did not suffice. He had even used her address once, he confessed, but had intentionally botched the zip code so nothing mailed to him would reach her. He carried a copy of his birth certificate these days, since identification had become more of an issue in the Homeland Security era, and he wrote that he had a passport, a piece of whimsy that amused Ellen no end. He had no resources on which to leave the country, and had never expressed a desire. In fact he had once written that, "The U.S. is all I need."

"Dear Heart, I am islanded by land! Far from you, far from the sea, missing both. I feel empty and parched, a man too long without sustenance. Has it really been twelve years since we last held hands, as your letter insisted, as we did in that restaurant booth in Philadelphia, both aching for what we have so sensibly decided we should never again have?" Ellen took a sip of coffee and considered that. Had they decided? They had, she guessed, decided they were not going to find an easy common ground. Nor would she leave her family for him, except in her fantasies perhaps. But had that led to giving up any hope of their having any connection other than this epistolary one? She wasn't sure.

"Today I am in Montana, having stopped in Idaho to work a while, and see an old friend. Your letter, which I plucked from my Missoula mailbox today, has been here a few weeks, I gather. I'm a little behind my schedule, not that I have ever promised clockwork reliability. The only thing that makes me sad about this is that if I was more on time I'd have gotten your letter sooner and I would have had sooner the lift it gave me now. Charitable friends near Billings beckon with the lure of day-work, hot food, clean sheets. And I can give the J-lop a rest for a few days, drain her crankcase, and re-oil her. I know it's wrong to think of a car as a woman, but I am celibate as a stone these days (think of me when you dream, baby) and she attends my needs, moves me from place to place, provides me shelter, and gives my butt the only bouncing it gets anymore. Hence I feminize and anthropomorphize. I hope you'll forgive with whatever small piece of you is not feminist this retrograde locution. I met the husband where I'm headed in Seattle years ago (at a wild party, but that's another story) and we became friends. His only objectionable habits in my book are that he works too hard, spends money on motorized things he doesn't need

– sports cars most notably – and he has an affinity for semi-automatic guns."

She thought about Richard's letter style, consistent since his first postcard, nearly thirty years ago, always compressed, always a playful edge of flirtation and apology, mixed with a touch of bragging. He trusted his choices like few people she knew, and this was part of why he still got to her so deeply. She wondered what he really looked like now. Even years ago, when she had last seen him, he had looked totally out of fashion, long hair, too much soft weight at forty. Now, at fifty, if his style hadn't changed, and nothing in his letters suggested it had, he would be a dinosaur, probably a heavy one. His weight, his size, had been part of what attracted her to him from the beginning. He was imposing, over six feet, over two hundred pounds, but there was such a touching gentleness, a need for care, that she had wanted him almost the first time they met. That it took several months for them to engineer their way into bed still astounds her, and also that it all got so fucked up at the end. Even the fact that eventually Paul and Richard had basically reconciled, become tolerant of each other if not friendly, had not saved it.

"Have been several places where I have thought of you. On a drive through the southeast of Utah I saw endless real estate of such unimaginable beauty I wished you were with me to see it. You are still the only woman I've ever known who could stand still in a landscape and take it the way an artist does. There are colors so strange they can only exist in nature, shapes so majestic an old barbarian like me is forced to think of God. Sometimes I imagine you on my road trips, not thinking about how we'd negotiate the day-to-day realities, but thinking how it would be to be able to turn to you and know you saw what I was seeing and that it would require no commentary. Oh God, I wish for that sometimes, for the luxury of not having to narrate, even to myself, why I love a sky or a valley so much. Will it surprise you to know that I talk aloud in the car so as not to lose my mind? But if I can imagine you there, there never seems to be the need. Not that talking wouldn't give me pleasure. It would, beyond imagining. But you are one of the only other sapiens I have ever met whose receiver seems permanently tuned to the same wavelengths as mine. Then I think, if you were here, that it'd ruin you, the things you were built for, the worldly success, the esteem the world has for you, and your need for it. How could I replace those things? You may be the last good woman on earth, El, and I hope that bozo you bunk with knows what it is he's got."

Years ago, after Richard had hit the road after his angry confrontation with Paul, she had asked him not to court her in letters anymore. It had become too painful and too confusing. The hurt was too close, then. Later she missed it and finally when the courting found its way back into his letters she did not object. "There is one thing I truly regret in the way I live. I wish sometimes that I had a kid. I envy you that, as I have said before. Your Ray, I wish was fruit of my loins, flesh of my flesh. And gawd, all his energy and grace. I saw his company perform in Tacoma, two Balanchine pieces, and a Forsythe study. I wish I was dad to that. I vowed to myself that if I ever had the chance, I'd do better than my parents, so much better. What will there be for me, what comfort, when I can no longer maintain the illusion that there is always a place to move on to? What will I have to show for my footloose decades?"

One of the baristas interrupted her reading to wipe down the table next to her. It was time to head back to work. She was working on a project to redevelop an old hospital into apartments. There were problems she had to solve – structural aspects of the building that prevented their just gutting the thing and rebuilding it inside. They had to work around the placement of certain beams and joists, and that always made redesign difficult and interesting. She wondered if Richard would be at all interested in the particulars of what she did for a living. She could imagine him arguing with her if she told him that she felt at her best, at her most creative, when she solved a problem in the original design of a building that had been created by someone else years ago. He would say that she had never really allowed herself to be her best, which is what you become when you are beholden to nothing and able to go anywhere or do anything you choose. She knew she protected herself from his judgment of her job by internalizing what she assumed would be his feeling about it, and so when she talked about what she did she downplayed it, made it sound somehow secondary, even temporary, the expected outcome of all the schooling, but providing her nothing so significant as self-worth or power. Though it did provide those things, and had for years. At the time of their last meeting, she had just been made partner in the architecture firm she had joined right out of grad school, but he did not ask what that would mean for her life. He saw her in relation to him, in relation to her husband and son, in relation to the fantasy that she might, one day, chuck it all and race across the country into his arms. For him, her job, like her family, was an impediment to the reality of their connection. To Richard, freedom was power, and he had been remarkably consistent in exercising it.

Although she had been there long enough to have read it all, there remained another page of the letter, and then a page of doodles. But Ellen felt exhausted. She skimmed to the end, stopping to read the captions on his crude drawings of roadside signs ("Artichoke Capital of Oregon!") and views he had seen. He had a flair for depicting a single element in a landscape to show its prominence, how it caught his attention, but he had no sense of perspective and his foreground and background collapsed into a kind of Egyptian-style frieze in which small birds and lizards might be the same size as cars or mountains. Still, the drawings made her smile, made her feel like she had some idea where he was.

The last time they had made love he had drawn in ink on her heels. The drawing tickled but she held still until he was through and then curled her leg around so she could see his work. "This is just a cheap way for you to get an unobstructed look between my legs," she told him as he watched her. The drawings were all coupling stick figures, in various exotic positions. "A poor man's *Kama Sutra*," she said. "Poor woman's," he corrected. "And portable." She turned back to the last page of the letter and read his itinerary. The closest he would be to Philadelphia was Boulder, Colorado, where he had some friends. She wondered if he ever came east anymore, if he came and didn't tell her, preferring the uncomplicated connection they had to the messy one that had preceded it. The last paragraph said, "I don't get to see many movies but a friend sat me down in front of the video of *Down and Out in Beverly Hills* because he said Nick Nolte reminded him of me. Even at my best, I don't see the resemblance. I didn't get the comparison except for the outsider stuff (I certainly don't resemble him – he's handsome even when he's a mess) but I realized that if that's what people I call my friends think of me, then there almost isn't a soul out there who really gets me. But I know you do. I love you. Take care. Think of me. Write soon. Yours." As usual, he did not sign his name.

Back at work, she pulled the file that had the rest of Richard's letters from her file drawer. They were in a manila expandable file, about four inches thick, with an elastic band around it. She thought again about what would happen if they were accidentally discovered by her secretary or one of her co-workers, rummaging for photocopies of elevations or ground plans for something. "Letters from an old friend," she would say, meaning an old difficulty, an old impossibility.

After she put the new letter and card in the folder and replaced it in her drawer, she scanned her desk. Her desk was covered with the blueprints for the hospital conversion.

Her work was to make the problems of brick and mortar appear to be advantages. She could do this. Her eyes moved as if by instinct to the elements in the plans that she would have to work around, reminding her that the important work did not leave her mind, even when she was not consciously thinking about it.

LOST THEN FOUND

What happened didn't break us, but it could have. I set her off. Without meaning to, but I did. Then I watched in horror her slow motion collapse. Like seeing a crack in a dam. First a trickle, then a flood. On the downstream side, everything uprooted, churning, then in the aftermath, a muddy calm. I was stunned, too slow to react. Correctly. Appropriately. I know this wasn't the time she would have chosen to tell me if I hadn't started her down that road. I couldn't have guessed what I was shaking loose, but that doesn't matter. Or excuse it. It's what I always seem to do. Blundering in. Charging ahead.

We were in bed, our first time, after an evening of gourmet take-out and talk. We were telling each other our life stories, more detailed versions of things we said on our first few dates, filling in places left sketchy before. We'd been taking it slow, being cautious with each other. I was excited when she invited me to her place. I'd brought the food and wine, things I thought would please her, the empty take out trays abandoned now on the coffee table in her living room, glazed with the remains. Bacon wrapped asparagus with buffalo mozzarella pillows. White bean and Italian sausage salad. Shrimp and scallop spring rolls, a double order. Duck Lyonnais salad with hard-cooked egg and cherry tomatoes. Spoon and finger foods to share. Things I thought she'd like, based on our earlier dates.

We met at choir practice, a community chorale that does a concert every spring, but rehearses year round. Those rehearsals filled a big void for me. It's hard to have a social life that doesn't involve drinking or sports, two things I'm not partial to. The choir has open auditions; I sang a show tune, one of my favorites from an old Bob Merrill show, *Carnival*. Jerry Orbach sang the original and I modeled my phrasing on his. "I've got to find a reason, for living on this earth." My tenor isn't bad, but I had no idea what I was doing. Everyone else was singing lieder or art songs. I was just glad they took me. Some of the members sing other places, church choirs or community theater musicals.

When this – what do I call it, conversation? – happened, I was just beginning to get a bigger picture of Addie's life. I knew she worked for Wells Fargo in the mortgage department. I knew her parents were dead, but that she had a brother and sister she rarely saw. She told me some stories about them when they were younger, like the fact that they performed Broadway musicals together for their parents. In those living room shows, she told me she was a bully about singing the big numbers, whether they were supposed to be for her character or not. She learned the songs from records she played over and over. I had done the same thing as a kid, listening to *Camelot* and *The King and I* and *My Fair Lady* until my parents regretted getting them for me.

I noticed that she had a guitar on a stand when I first came into her apartment, set up like she was rehearsing for something. I made a joke about Maria von Trapp. There was a small upright piano in the corner too. She hadn't mentioned that she played either on our earlier dates. I was hoping maybe we could sing together at some point. She sometimes sang solos with the choir; she had a terrific voice.

Her apartment was classy, furnished in a Danish modern style that all looked like it would be uncomfortable but surprisingly turned out not to be. Her place looked like one of those sample units I sometimes see through the ground floor windows of rehabbed buildings, perfectly furnished to entice potential tenants. Her instruments made the place feel lived in. There was sheet music open on the piano, and music books on the bench. There was a small electronic tuning device, a capo, and a handful of guitar picks scattered on the coffee table. But other than that, until I introduced chaos in the form of the take out trays, her place was neat as a pin. When I came in she told me to put my coat anywhere, but I felt funny about dumping it on the back of a chair like I would at home. I hung it on the doorknob of what of course turned out to be a coat closet.

In the lull that followed her telling me about singing as a kid I said, "I finally got around to checking you out on Facebook. You post a lot of pictures of pies." I thought I was being cute, showing her I was interested in her baking hobby or habit or whatever it was. I watched her face fall.

"I don't know how I feel about that."

"I'm not judging you. Pies are pretty sexy."

"Not exactly what I mean."

"You don't think I should have checked you out? Get a little leg up on the insider stuff? Anticipate your likes and dislikes. Visualize your friends and family. Isn't that what everyone does now-a-days? Especially when they start dating?" I felt a fogy alarm go off in my head when I said "now-a-days" and "dating."

"That's why I don't like it. Don't you want to learn those things on your own?"

"How about making sure you aren't a serial killer? Or don't have stalker former boyfriends who might threaten me."

"I don't think you'll find evidence of my murderous side on Facebook. Don't they block stuff like that?"

"I Googled you, too."

"Really? You know all my secrets, then."

"You have lots of friends."

"If you think that, you don't know me at all."

"I stalked you and counted." I expected her to laugh at that. When she didn't I said, "Actually, you ought to check your security. Anyone can find you."

I saw the look of concern pass over her face. She told me, "I'm pretty much of a Luddite when it comes to this. My brother set up that stuff ten years ago. I haven't had any friend requests in ages. Some people from work, maybe two years ago. The rest were mostly girl friends from college, one or two people I stay in touch with from high school, and the aunts and nieces my brother friended for me when I first got on. I don't really want everyone knowing the same things about me, so I don't post much. A few pictures from vacations. And yes, the pies. When they come out perfect. I'm pretty vain about my baking. But that's it. Nothing personal really, ever."

"I'm actually a very big fan of pie, in case you want to file that away for future reference. Apple and sour cherry. With crumble on top, if you really want me to be your love slave forever."

I hadn't had a serious relationship in a while, and I wanted this one to work. With hindsight, I was probably pushing too hard, but it didn't feel like I was in the moment. We were the same age, fifty-two, and we had a lot of the same reference points. Music and world events. Our first few dates hadn't been exactly awkward, but it wasn't like sparks flew, either. But in the absence of other prospects, we stuck it out, through over-long conversations about movies and books, about which we generally agreed, shorter ones about politics, about which we didn't always. Now, six weeks in, it finally felt to me like we might be going somewhere. I'd been lonely so long it was nice to feel like I could still get this far in a relationship without saying or doing something stupid enough to scare the other person off. I had begun to have my doubts. And I genuinely liked her, which may seem like the baseline for a relationship having any sort of traction, let alone long-term potential, but when you've been out of the groove as long as I have it turns out that it's sometimes hard to know quickly what's what. I'm not a man who has ever experienced love at first sight, and

66

I've dated enough women I've liked fine on the first date and haven't by the third, that I tend to reserve judgment. And more women than I would like to admit have stopped returning my calls after a few dates because we simply didn't click. But with Addie and me, there was some chemistry. Or I felt there was.

"I know people who post all the time," she said after a moment. "Not only their own pictures, but videos that are supposed to make you feel good. It's just that not everything that's supposed to make you feel good actually does."

Something had shifted. I heard it in her voice, but I didn't want to think it meant anything. I was enjoying myself, feeling a little flip, showing off. It had been so long since I had gotten to do that. Things were clicking. Then she moved her body, scooting slightly away from me. When I reached for her, she shook me off. I thought maybe my hand was cold, so I retracted it. Nothing was natural yet; nothing was exactly settled in, the way a couple that was more experienced with each other might have been. When she started talking again, the subject was still the Internet. I thought we were going on from where we were, but we weren't.

"One of my co-workers, Camille, posted a video of a class playing *Amazing Grace* on instruments they made out of junk they got from a landfill. Everyone knows the song, of course." She sang the most famous line. "'I once was lost and now I'm found, I was blind, but now I see.' They were from a school in Vermont, from a town I never heard of. Pitchfield?"

"Never heard of it, either."

"The classroom had a slightly bedraggled look to it, like it hadn't been painted in a while. And no one had thought to tell the kids to dress up for the video, which I admit was kind of endearing at first. 'Here we are, just playing this song for you,' you know? They were clearly pleased with themselves, holding up their instruments for the camera at the end of song, big smiles on their faces. Their teacher had turned a music lesson into a lesson about recycling, and you could see that they were having a good time showing off for the camera."

"Sounds like a video destined to go viral."

"I have no idea how that happens. Camille's the only person whose posts are things like that. She likes the ones that are supposed to make you tear up, the cop who gives away money dressed like Santa, the kid with brain cancer who gets in the game in the final seconds and shoots the winning basket."

"I like the inter-species friendship ones, the hippo nuzzling a tortoise, the cat licking the macaw. Click bait."

"Right. The caption on the one Camille sent was, 'You Won't Believe what this Great Teacher had his Kids Do.' So I bit. Then I almost closed it before it was done. I wish I had. I really don't know why I watched to the end. They didn't slaughter the song, but the playing wasn't special in any way, and the instruments were exactly what you would expect from eighth graders making banjos and xylophones out of junk. The kids were bunched together in the front of the classroom facing the camera and while they were playing they cut in some shots of when they gathered stuff from the landfill. The teacher had his back to the camera, standing in the middle of the room, conducting. At the very end, he turned toward the camera for less than a second. It was enough. I recognized him."

"You recognized him? That's bizarre. Who was he?"

At first I wasn't sure if she was going to tell me. I thought maybe it was an old flame, something like that. She was weighing it, and I thought, and almost said, that she didn't need to protect me, that I would be okay with whoever it was. Then she made the decision and tossed it out. "He was the person who raped me at summer camp, thirty-six years ago. When I was sixteen."

I wanted to believe that I hadn't heard her right, but I knew I had. It took me a moment to realize that the ringing in my ears was not outside my head. Everything seemed suddenly out of whack, and nothing that came out of my mouth in the moments afterward was right or appropriate or useful. It was a bumble, sounds that signified nothing.

"You're kidding. You're not serious. I really don't know....I can't imagine....I don't know what to say." I shut up.

"For a moment, right afterward, I wasn't sure what I'd seen. It seemed unlikely it was him. I was jiggling my mouse side to side, trying to decide if I wanted to know for sure, or if it was better to let it go and assume I was mistaken. I thought maybe I had a moment of panic because of a vague resemblance. Or maybe I was simply deluded."

"Tell me you didn't replay it." I was pleading against something I already understood she had done.

"Why?" She let the question linger. I don't think she was being mean. I think she was asking if I wanted to go on, if I wanted to hear the rest. I had no answer to the actual question. If I said, "So you wouldn't have to know that he was out there, that he was leading his life," I was saying that I hoped she could find a way to deny what she knew. If I said, "Because it would hurt you," she might understand I was more sensitive to her pain, but she would also likely get the message that I really thought it best if she was over it for the sake of our future relationship. But I wasn't clear about my hesitation then. I was just stuck. I wanted to say the right thing, and I knew I wasn't.

She shifted in the bed again, pulling farther away from me. "I didn't click replay immediately. Camille, of course, had no idea who the teacher in the video was, if he even was who I thought he was. How could she? She didn't know me in high school. She didn't go to the summer camp. We never talked about our pasts at all. I think the most I know about her is that she sees her mother once a week and has a boyfriend she thinks is unreliable but has been with forever. Mark, maybe, or Mac. The most she knew about me other than work stuff was that I sing in a choir."

"Addie, are you sure you want to tell me about this?"

"You don't want to hear it? It's okay if you don't. I mean, I'd understand."

"I do. I want you to tell me what you need to tell me. I just want to understand, why now? I mean here and now?"

"Because it came up. Because it's on my mind. Maybe it's always on my mind and I just forget it sometimes. Maybe it was what you said about Facebook. I'm sorry. Look, I think our relationship is headed somewhere. You feel that too, right? It doesn't seem like this is a one-night thing? So I want you to know. I guess for some men I've known, men our age, if they find out someone they're getting serious about has this in her past, it becomes...I don't know. It's just what's happened before. It becomes a deal breaker. They can't get past it."

"You think it would be for me? I hope you don't think...."

"What?"

"I could be...like him. Like any man for whom it would be a 'deal breaker.' Anything like that." I was trying to be steady, and to let her know it, but I was also stung by the implication of what she said, and this was out before I had a chance to consider how it sounded.

She said, "I'm not good at this. I don't know when I should tell it. It doesn't seem like a first date conversation. Or a second. But if I let it go too long, and then I tell the story, it seems like I was hiding it. I wanted to go to bed with you. I did. But it was in my mind the whole time that I hadn't told you yet, that it might not be something you'd want to do if you knew."

"Addie." She turned away from me. I thought she might be crying, but I was afraid to reach too forcefully for her. "It's okay. I'm sorry. I wish I knew what else.... I'm sorry you were hurt like that."

She waved her hand to shut me down. "As hard as I tried to convince myself that it was probably not him, I knew it was. That he had become a music teacher in some Podunk Vermont school. I knew it was him."

She sat up and turned further away from me. I touched her back. "If there's more, tell me the rest." I wasn't sure this was the right thing to say, but I knew I couldn't just let it go. The only way out of the conversation seemed to be through it. And there was another thing. I really did like her, and I felt like I needed to know. To get past it if we were going to go forward together, or to cauterize it if we needed to do that, or, if it was going to finish us, I wanted some indication before I left her bed. Then she got out of bed and put on a robe, tied it tight around her, and sat in the chair facing the bed. I felt imprisoned there, and suddenly uncomfortably naked. I looked around for my clothes, which were strewn around her room. I wanted to be dressed, to be sitting with her anywhere but in that bed. But there was no graceful way out of it.

"The place it happened was really beautiful, a music camp for kids in the Adirondacks. I heard about it from someone at school who made it sound magical, so I begged my parents to let me go. I could hardly believe it when they said yes. They were so protective. I overheard my father arguing with my mother about it. 'Let her go,' he said. 'She's so enthusiastic about it. It'll be a great experience.'"

"My cabin mates and I were all so full of ourselves. We actually talked about what kinds of artists we were going to be. Some of them were already virtuosos. A few of the actors, kids from New York City, had been in professional shows, and some of the girls were so beautiful you knew they could be stars. We bunked together by age, but we were assigned to activities as 'majors.' We took lessons and practiced. The main idea of the place was that music was a communal experience. Communal experiences were a big idea there. You came to camp, you shared everything. Living space. Chores. Performance. The only thing we did alone was practice.

"There was a regular routine. Classes followed by practice time in the morning. Physical activities and swimming followed by practice time in the afternoon. Concerts and shows after dinner. The first week, the faculty performed. They did hard stuff, too, scenes from absurdist plays, movements from modern symphonies, full concertos, big work. After that, it was up to us. The jazz majors improvised on standard scores. The arts kids put up their work around the barn where performances took place. The orchestra played symphonies. The theater kids mounted plays. We showed our best to each other; that was the point. It was like a Brigadoon. For a month every summer, rising out of the mists of the Adirondacks. Thirty days later – poof. Gone. Back into the earth.

"I came to camp as a guitar major. A folk musician. I learned the guitar because I had a good voice. I loved to sing and I wanted to be able to accompany myself, and also I suppose because by sixteen I cut the figure. Long blond hair I let go stringy, a little bit of Joni Mitchell, a little bit of Mary Travers.

"The way Leonard Cohen and Bob Dylan were for me. We were born too late."

"I wore their records down. I wanted to be like them, do what they did. So much freedom. I heard it when they sang. I saw it in the pictures on their album covers. Joni Mitchell standing naked near the ocean, singing about her lovers, how she knew her heart and mind even when her men were jerks. Before the rape, I used to imagine myself on stage singing. Spotlight, big, adoring crowds. The whole deal. It was not the only way I was naïve."

"Do you still sing those songs?"

"I sing, but other than in choir, not usually so anyone can hear. I joined the choir so I could use my voice. I almost quit the first time I got offered a solo."

"I'm glad you didn't. I'd love to hear you sing some Joni Mitchell sometime."

"We'll see." There was a long pause, and then she said, "I'm a little cold. Would you mind?"

She came back to bed, but leaned into me from outside of the sheet and blanket I was under. She maneuvered into a position where she was in contact, and slid down in the bed, and folded her legs up next to mine, but she felt miles away. And I had such mixed feelings about what was happening. On the one hand, I wanted to hear the story. On the other, I understood that this meandering route was the only one she could take. She was not telling me something she knew how to tell. It was unfolding the way it occurred to her to tell it, not directly or clearly, but by a more organic logic.

"I marvel at the people who came out of camp and did what they set out to do. Some have been successful their whole lives. One of the beautiful girls in my cabin was Mari Antinoff. You know who that is right?"

"Sure. She was there?"

"She had major parts off-Broadway by the time we were eighteen. I still see her picture in *The New York Times* a couple of times a year. She has that facial structure that looked great at sixteen, and just keeps getting better as she ages. Like Blythe Danner, or Jane Fonda. *The New Yorker* did a profile on her a few years ago. She's always on television."

"I read that profile. Didn't she say something about the camp?"

"She did. How going there helped her figure out who she was, what she wanted to do. How lucky that was." I waited for her to say something else, something angry or ironic about luck, but she didn't. "A lot of the musicians who were there at the same time as I was went on to play in major bands or orchestras. Mary Netsky wrote that anti-war song, *Melting Down the Guns*. She was in the next older cabin. Her best friend was Hallie Paul, the ABC News correspondent."

"I know who she is. She was wounded in Iraq, right?"

"Hallie and I were bunkmates. We weren't exactly friends. She was a kind of social butterfly, part of a large group of kids who always seemed to be doing the coolest things. They were the kids who organized their own late night cabarets, who were always sneaking cigarettes when the counselors weren't looking. I'd been smoking since I was fifteen, and one of the reasons that I got to know Hallie was she bummed smokes from me. The main thing I knew about her was that she was sort of going out with the guy who raped me, though 'going out' is not exactly the right description. They were an obvious camp crush. 'Out' was the out-of-doors. No one went off the grounds or ever thought to. The grounds were vast. There were acres of woods, and finding a place to make out in the dark was hardly difficult.

"A few years back I read that book called *The Interestings*. It starts with kids at an arts camp. There's a rape in it, too. The kids in that book had the same expectations of their futures we did. When I read it, it made me wonder if rape was a common thing in places where there's minimal supervision and the kids thought they were special. Artists aren't supposed to inflict pain on each other. It goes against the whole idea. They don't hurt each other, or force sex on each other. "

"I don't think that makes them immune."

"When I was thirteen, after my father had become successful, he bought a speedboat that he loved to race around Schroon Lake. He rented a slip there. For my brother and sister those rides were so horrible they eventually stopped going out with him. For me they were liberating. I loved my hair whipping in the wind, and the lightness in my chest when the boat leapt out of the water speeding over a wake. Where my brother clutched the seat in sheer terror, I raised my hands over my head in total delight. I knew he would never do anything to put me in danger. For years after it happened, my father asked me why I stopped singing. I couldn't tell him. He would have blamed himself. He would have thought he had sent me someplace where I wasn't safe."

I realized she was crying. I reached across the bed for a tissue, and I stroked her hair as she blew her nose. "It took a good deal of therapy to actually believe that I did not bring the rape on myself or set something in motion that turned into something I didn't want, or any of the other stupid things people say about how these things happen." I knew there was nothing to say, but I wanted to say things, like not to blame herself, which is what it sounded to me like she was doing, though saying anything would have probably sounded foolish.

"I was simply being nice, talking to another kid, walking home after a campfire. There were crowds of people around. Then suddenly there weren't and we were away from everyone, off the trail. I can't remember how we got there. Then he started kissing me. I was hesitant and eager at the same time, flattered and surprised. He was tall and good looking, confident and sly. One of the cool kids. Did he ask me whether it was all right that he kissed me? I think he did. That was all the permission I gave. But then he was being rough, and he was holding me against a tree and then his hands were up my shirt and then my shorts were down. He put his tongue in my mouth pressed his mouth so hard into me I could hardly breathe. And then he entered me. He was fierce and menacing, and whatever no I was feeling, I could not say it. It was shocked out of me, the impulse and the ability all at once, and I was taken, simply taken, in a moment. And then it seemed too late to protest, too late to complain, too late to blame anyone but myself for having gone up the path with him, for having believed that he just wanted to walk me back to my cabin.

"Afterward, when the world became molasses, when I was dazed and it was as if I was moving through mud and fog, I could not even remember the details clearly. They were jumbled up. What I said, what he said. If I had been asked to, I couldn't have testified to anything with certainty. At camp, things went on as if they were normal, as if I was. I did everything anyone expected me to do. I learned new songs. I performed them on my showcase night. People applauded and praised my singing and playing. But I was not there. Something just shut down. Something was broken. Some part of me was gone.

"Nothing that I did after that, now that we know more about rape and its aftermath, was far from the normal, if self-degradation and shame can be considered normal. I was detached and sad. I spent the senior year of high school cutting classes and hiding from everyone. No one seemed to notice. Whatever expectations anyone had had of me before the rape, after it they gradually let those expectations go, as if there was some unspoken agreement that what I became was all I could be. My teachers behaved indifferently to my presence, and indifferently to my absences. I spent hours in my room playing my guitar, at which I got quite good, good enough to get into the Baxter School of Music for college. My parents mistook diligence for devotion, assumed it was what I chose. But it wasn't. It was the only thing I could do. I comforted myself with music, and later with sex. Six months after my rape, I emerged from my cocoon and went on a tear, letting boys do whatever they wanted with me. I was partial to boys who were somewhat fey, who did not feel physically strong or threatening, who saw sex with me as a gift. Did I want to control them? To assert some principle of pleasure in my life? The rape had been negligibly painful, not searing in a physical way, just unwanted, unwelcomed.

He invaded my mind as much as my body. For a while, I convinced myself that anyone taking my virginity would have hurt me as much. I also convinced myself to be flippantly grateful that I did not have to go through the agony of bad first-time sex with a boy whose heart I would eventually break. Or who would have broken mine.

"I made it through a year of college before it completely caught up. I spent a summer being a disaster cliché, drinking, drugging, and eventually collapsing. And then nothing I had done before seemed possible to do ever again, not playing, not singing, not anything."

Addie got out of bed at this point and went to the bathroom and shut the door. I thought about getting dressed, but I didn't want her to think I was leaving. I wanted to get out of the bed, but I didn't want to suggest I was uncomfortable holding her if it was her intention to return there. I heard the toilet flush, and then the sink go on and off, and then I saw the light go out under the bathroom door. It took her a minute to open the door and come back into the bedroom. She had washed her face. It hadn't really registered that she was wearing makeup before, but now, washed away, she looked different, paler, sadder. She got back into bed, in the same place, on top of the covers next to me.

"Do you mind this? I feel like I have to tell you the rest now. I feel bad I started this. I feel like I ruined your night."

"I'm not going anywhere. Tell me what you need to tell me." I reached out and took her hand. She let me, but withdrew it after a few moments.

"Sorry," she said. "I'm almost done. Just let me finish, okay?"

"Of course. Yes."

"So, Camille saw me at work the day after she posted the video of my rapist conducting his ersatz orchestra, and she asked me if I liked it. I was completely thrown by the question. She didn't usually ask about the things she sent; they were uninvited gifts I usually felt I didn't need to respond to. But that day, when I barely made it in to the office, she waited for me to validate her for sending it. I was dumbstruck. My options for responding seemed remarkably similar to what happened after rape – acknowledge it in some way, be outraged by it, or bury it. Camille meant no harm. She thought she was doing a good deed, brightening my day. So after a moment I said, 'Cute. Very cute.'"

"I have thought about the boy who raped me and the man he turned into many times over the years. Once, some years back, when I had a steady boyfriend with whom a future looked possible, I decided I should to tell him what had happened to me, and that although I felt there were no lasting effects, I could not be sure what might set me off. I wanted to explain the bouts of sadness he had already witnessed. At that point, more than one therapist had suggested my issues threaded themselves back to the unresolved issues of anger I had about being violated. After I told him my story he asked me, 'What would you say to him if you could see him now?' I didn't know how to answer. I couldn't tell him that when I felt most angry, I sometimes imagined something violent happening to him."

"Sexually violent?"

"Abstractly violent. Not something I cause. Like he's hit by a truck. Maybe I thought about more specific retribution right after it happened. But I don't anymore. One of the therapists I saw suggested I try to find a way to forgive myself for all the things I blamed myself for doing wrong."

"That sounds like more self-blame. You should quit that. I know, that's easy for me to say. But I hope you have."

"I don't know. I guess I have. Mostly. I didn't obsess about it until I saw the video, and even now, it's not in the front of my thoughts. Most of the time.

"But it's present enough that you felt you wanted to tell me."

"Yes. Because...." There was a long pause. "Because it defined me. Because I became a woman who was raped. Because I was a child who was. However sophisticated I thought I was back then, I was a child."

"Does that matter? Would it have been any less awful if you had been eighteen or twenty-five or fifty?"

"I guess not. Sometimes I think I might...that things might have gone differently afterward."

"I wish I had known you then. Before, I mean. I wish I could have been there to protect you."

"I've heard that before. I know this is going to sound mean, but it doesn't help to hear that."

"I'm sorry."

"Everyone wishes bad things didn't happen. It's how we go on from things that frighten us, but are not ours to feel. And please stop saying you're sorry. That doesn't help either. I know that's another awful thing to say. But I need you to."

"It's okay."

It was a long time before she spoke again, long enough for everything about the evening to dissolve slightly. For a moment, sitting next to her, I did not know who she was, what I was doing there, how I had gotten there, or how I would move ahead in my life. I felt like I was under water, like we were, like a swirling current was carrying us, clutched together, and we did not know whether or where we would land. The flood after the breaking of the dam. I did not know if I could get out of that bed, and I did not know if she wanted me there. I did not want to move, and at the same time I wanted to be anywhere else in the world. Then she said, "You know what I hope? How I would answer the question that guy asked if someone asked it now? I'd say I hope he grew up to be a better man than he was a boy. I think that's why I did it. Why I watched the video again. To see if I could see that."

I found the video of the teacher on line the day after our conversation, though I never told Addie I watched it. I wanted to see him, to see if he was worthy of her generosity, or deserving of my anger. I played it several times, pausing at the moment he turned to face the camera, sheepishly taking credit for his good deed with the kids he was teaching. I stared at his face, studied it. In the end, it held nothing revealing. He was normal looking, not monstrous, not what I wanted him to be. I fantasized driving up to Pitchfield and lying in wait for him, jumping him from behind and beating him near enough to death that he suffered pain every day he lived after that. There was a large part of me that wanted to do it. In more rational moments, I thought of trying to get Facebook to take down his video. Of course, I did neither. I doubt Addie would have wanted me to. There was nothing heroic for me to do, even invisibly. But he haunted me, that bastard, and I wished him harm. I could not muster one iota of the generosity Addie had. I hated him, and the impact of his selfish violence on her, on her world. And all these years later, on mine.

At the end of telling me the story of her rape, Addie asked me what I thought of the hymn. I said I thought it was all right, that other than in choir, I wasn't the hymn-singing type. Addie said, "I used to love that hymn. It's a redemption story, you know. Written by a slave trader who had a conversion experience. I am not a believer, but I used to sing it when I needed to feel hopeful."

I sometimes wish that she had not told me. That our story had gone on without my knowing, without going in that direction on that night, in that moment, like I came to wish she had not turned off the path and followed that boy into the darkness that night, years ago, on her way up to her cabin at the arts camp. It's a naïve idea, wishing to change things that actually happened, though I embrace it none-the-less. As I embrace the idea that knowing the source of her pain, my love might be enough to overcome it.

80

THE ABUNDANCE LEAGUE

Before Tuesday, February 26, 2013, Steve Tedesco considered himself pretty much of a chump. Luck had never been his lady. Then, on that day, Steve opened his mailbox to a single envelope, the notification of the upcoming *Periodical Power! Sweepstakes*, no purchase required to enter. He was laid off from the *Abundance Food Markets* chain during the economic downturn. They decided to go with meats cut and pre-packaged at a central distribution center rather than having butchers pack individual cuts in the stores. They even tried to fool the customers by making the packaging look exactly like it always had, with styrene trays wrapped in clear plastic wrap and what looked like store-generated price stickers. Since the layoff, Steve barely ate any meat. "Who can afford meat? No one can afford it," the men on the *Abundance* bowling league team had commiserated, some of them facing layoffs as well.

Before his layoff, when notices of sweepstakes came in the mail a couple of times a year, he ignored them, assuming they were bogus or that with his luck his downstairs neighbor would win and not him. Now, in what he immediately recognized was a hopefulness born out of desperation, the promise that "you might already have won" gave him an occasion to dream about having a little spendable cash not committed to rent and utilities. He tucked the envelope into his pocket thinking "what the hell." He had an afternoon with nothing else to do, and who knew? At that moment it seemed no less a crapshoot than his job search did.

As he climbed the stairs back to his apartment he drooled a little thinking about what he would do with a little extra money. He would buy some decent steaks. His two favorite cuts were New York strip and sirloin. On the job, he had sometimes used his fifteen percent employee discount to buy a twenty-four ounce strip, or a beautiful prime sirloin of the same size, a manly portion but not beyond him, particularly if he had nothing to do the next day. Sometimes eating a big steak made him a little logy, especially if he also nuked himself a potato to go along with it.

The sweepstakes envelope was full of enticements. Cheap magazine subscriptions, the reason for the sweepstakes, with special deals for the first year and even better deals for multi-year subscriptions. Also templates for bank checks with pictures of the Grand Canyon and other national monuments on them, or "your own photos here" checks, on which one could have snapshots of dogs or kids or anything else printed. Steve had neither kids nor a dog. He wondered if anyone even wrote checks anymore. If even schlubs like him did his banking electronically, it was hard to imagine that anyone actually sent hand written payments through the mail. The post office was laying people off, his friend Damian had told him, and the fact that no one was paying by check was probably the reason.

Deeper in the sweepstakes mailer there were also deals for term life insurance at "pennies at day." "Like that's what I'm gonna do with my unemployment," he said aloud. He thought, but did not say, who would they pay it to? Steve's wife had left him. She had made his life miserable, and he was going to be damned if she got anything from his death. She would probably be partially to blame if he dropped dead tomorrow. He started smoking when things started going bad with her, and besides, he reasoned, she caused him enough grief to give any man a dozen heart attacks. Other than her, he had no one. His parents were dead, and his brother was an asshole he would never in a million years want to support after he was dead either.

At his kitchen table he pasted the "No Thanks" stickers in all the applicable places. He couldn't really afford to spend money on anything that might be deemed a luxury. Despite liking *Time* and *Field and Stream* and *Car and Driver* the last time he had picked them up in his dentist's office, magazines were not in the necessities category. He put the reply form back in the envelope, found a stamp, kissed the sealed envelope for luck, and tucked it carefully into his jacket pocket to mail when he went out.

Steve did not, in fact, much believe in his chances. He was distrustful of luck as an ordering force in the universe. One of his bowling buddies from the *Abundance* league once told him that he was the unluckiest guy he'd ever met. There were two reasons. Steve's ex-wife had once been homecoming queen, plain when compared to the women he saw fancied up in magazines, but a beauty in his neighborhood. He had loved her with a ferocity that often scared her. If he saw someone looking at her in a store or at the bowling alley in a way that seemed flirtatious, he would use his size to back the guy down. Steve was big, and though he was not muscular, his stature had a certain menace to it. Though no one had ever seen him throw a punch, there was a general belief that he was not the kind of guy you'd want to mess with. There was the fact that he was a butcher for one thing. People assumed that butchering made him dangerous, skilled at cutting up meat, and by extension, people. And there was the fact that he had ready access to cleavers and knives.

The problem was, his wife had gotten tired of him, and she had begun to flirt shamelessly with some of the other guys she saw every Wednesday at the *Abundance* bowling league games, who were also guys Steve worked with at the market. In fact, though he didn't know it until much later, when she taunted him with the information on her way out the door the night she left him for good, she had had quickies with a couple of guys Steve worked with, and had gone down on a third one in his car one night in the *Abundance* parking lot while she was waiting for Steve to get off his shift. But she had no intention of breaking off with one butcher to take up with another, or a deli man, or a dairy man either. She simply wanted to get Steve's goat, and she played him like a top seed plays an unranked pretender. She exhausted him with fakes and feints, and tortured him with innuendo and suspicion, then she flummoxed him with kindness until the night she slaughtered him with the truth. But until that night, she always went home with him.

After that, his bowling buddies decided he was unlucky, even though some of them knew the guys who had participated in the activities that had turned his luck sour and induced his wife to leave. But even the ones in relationships as precarious as Steve's knew they were staying put, and so what else to do but commiserate? They understood, those who had girlfriends or wives themselves, that they were all likely dull enough to be in jeopardy of boring their partners into quickies in some parking lot, if not outright desertion as well, and so they hung on, which was why they thought Steve was unlucky. He hadn't been able to hang on. The other men knew they were as likely to be left as he was, and so they did their grim jobs with the best humor they could muster, slicing deli or slicing cheese or stocking shelves with yogurt and milk and kefir. How many entertaining stories can a man bring home to his wife about what happens in the dairy aisle?

In addition to losing his wife and losing his job, Steve had a chronic skin condition that caused him to itch all the time. He hadn't had it all his life; it came on when he hit his mid-forties, a little harbinger of the physical decline he knew would get him in the end. Despite his ex-wife's caustic and debilitating behavior, Steve knew that it was less likely that he would have a dramatic coronary than a series of tiny conditions that would add up to a critical mass of stupid decay. Death by a thousand non-lethal ailments. Steve knew that he was headed down hill in every way. The things that had impressed girls in high school – his size contrasted with his native naiveté and his galumphing kindness – seemed freakish and even slightly creepy in a grownup. He knew he was easily duped and misled, and that he could hardly tell real need from trumped-up kindness meant to manipulate him. Even his luck as a bowler seemed to desert him after he turned forty-five and his score dropped thirteen points on average, which changed his handicap to an embarrassingly high one, the highest in the *Abundance* league.

So it was a hopeful but not totally believing man who dropped the sweepstakes envelope into the mail slot on a stroll to the Seven Eleven the same night the sweepstakes announcement had come in the mail, and it was the same disbelieving man who opened his door one morning six weeks later to a well-dressed man holding a giant fake check that had "One Million Dollars" written on it, which translated to about six hundred and sixty-one thousand when all the taxes were taken. This was, Steve recognized, an astonishing change of fortune.

The first people Steve heard from after the news of his sweepstakes win got around were his former store mates and bowling buddies from the *Abundance* league. A couple of them stopped over, ostensibly to congratulate him, but it soon became obvious that each of them had a proposal for Steve about how he might share in his luck. A business proposition from Len, a dairy counterman he did not really know all that well, to whom he had once given advice about buying a used car. A restaurant idea from Sully, the deli guy he sometimes ate lunch with back when he had been working, who had the same thing every day, tuna with tomato on rye, and hardly presented himself as the kind of guy from whom one might want to entertain a risky business proposal, let alone join in a partnership. Still, Steve listened politely to the man's pitch before he told him going into the restaurant business was not what he wanted to do with his new-found wealth. "Just think about it," Sully told him. "We'd be a great team."

Then he got a very sexy marriage proposal from Diya, a woman who worked in produce, who assured him that "even though we don't really know each other all that well now" – she had barely spoken to him before she came to see him after he won the sweepstakes – "I will treat you so well that you will surely learn to be in love with me. I would cook for you and I would manage your household," she told him, eyeing his less-than-immaculate apartment. "You could live like a king as long as you took care of me." He wondered if that meant indulging her taste for fashion accessories and jewelry. She was Indian, from Bangalore, and always wore layers of hanging necklaces and long earrings. She explained that her parents had an arranged marriage. "They had not even laid eyes on each other before their wedding day and for nearly forty years they have been completely satisfied and happy." She made it clear in the tone of her delivery what she meant by satisfied.

"Surely two people who know each other a little bit, who have shared the realities and absurdities of working in a retail grocery, especially if one of them is sexually attracted to the other, have at least as good a chance at happiness as my parents did." She did not specify which one was the attracted one and which one the attractive, and he did not ask. He told her he would think about it, intending never to let it cross his mind again.

When the actual money arrived (the big check was just for publicity; the shot they used on TV showed that Steve had come to the door in his bathrobe), he paid his bills and bought a new car, a red four-door Toyota Camry, though he drove a few hotter vehicles before he came to his senses. He thought about moving to a better apartment, but decided he liked the place he was living well enough and instead decided to get it painted and to buy a few new pieces of furniture and a new bed and call it a day. He bought a few new pairs of jeans from the Levis' website, and a new winter coat, which he desperately needed, on sale at a Burlington Coat Factory, and some other items like tee shirts and socks and underwear. He was smart enough to realize that six and a half hundred thousand bucks was not really enough money to go hog wild on, and that really if he was honest with himself about it, it was at best a decent cushion and not a lifetime guarantee. At about the same time, his unemployment ran out. He needed to find a job.

The state employment center, to which he had been reporting dutifully, had job placement services, and if a job like the one he had been relieved of came along, he was obliged to apply for it. But no butchers had ever been listed on the help wanted lists, and he would be damned if he was going to take a lesser retail job or a job stacking cereal or canned goods. "I have skills, and I like the work," he told the employment counselor when she suggested that given his size and stature he might want to look at building trades jobs or work as a security guard. "I was an apprentice butcher before I became a full-fledged butcher, and the company sent me to meat school, not to mention doing the job for all these years, and I feel like putting in all that time should count for something." The counselor nodded sympathetically, but reminded him that he was on a countdown and that his unemployment would run out very soon. The truth was that he had done the minimum looking during his unemployment, assuming that economic conditions would change over the months his unemployment ran, and he would eventually go back to butchering at *Abundance* once the recession ended. However, after weeks of nothing on offer he changed his mind. Something easier, less messy, less physically demanding, less hard to talk about at home at the end of the day with his partner – if he ever again had a partner – might actually make some sense. The idea began to appeal to him.

He began to think about Diya's proposal as well. He was five years shy of fifty, after all. How many opportunities would he have to find someone to share his life with? When he thought about dating or trying to find a woman in the local bar scene, the prospect seemed daunting and potentially humiliating. He began to imagine what living with Diya might be like, and he even allowed himself to fantasize about her as a sexual partner, since she had brought it up.

Eleven weeks after the actual sweepstakes check came, he got an interview to be the second shift manager at a food bank. The pay was not very good, about a third less than he had been making at *Abundance*, but he warmed quickly to the notion that he'd be management and not employee, and he liked the idea that he would be doing something good, something that helped people. The work itself had some challenges, paper work was not his forte, but he figured he could conquer that. He liked the people who interviewed him, and he liked the warehouse where large-scale food donations were collected and repackaged for individual distribution. It was clean, cleaner than the back room abattoir at *Abundance* had ever been. It was well lighted, and buzzing with people who seemed passionate about redistributing food to the poor. Some of them were the actual poor, working for or volunteering for the organization that had helped them when they had been struck low. When they made him a final offer, which included better health and retirement benefits than he had had at *Abundance*, if a lower salary, he took the job.

The morning he started his new job, Steve thought about his luck, if all of these changes meant it was changing, but he chased the notion from his mind. "Don't want to jinx it," he told himself, and forced himself to think about which tie he would wear.

His courtship of Diya started slowly. A coffee date, then movie dates, then dinner and movie, then a few nights with no entertainment agenda, just hanging out at his place or hers. They made out, but neither seemed to be in a hurry to take their physical relationship any further, and though surprised by the power of it, Steve had to admit he liked the affection they seemed to have for each other almost as much as he remembered liking sex. It felt good to be with a woman who wanted to be with him, even if the initial reason for it was something other than love. To Steve, they seemed to be compatible. They seemed to be headed somewhere.

Their first argument was about the job at the food bank. Diya did not think the food bank job was a good one. She did not think it paid enough, and she did not like that he got called in at odd hours to supervise the delivery or distribution of an unexpected gift of melons from a caterer who had overbought, or shepherd in a load of chicken wings from a restaurant that miscalculated. She was uncomfortable that she was making more money than he was. "It is not right. It can cause resentment in the future. The man should be the provider. He should make more." Steve was surprised at how traditional she was about sex roles and family dynamics. "I'm okay with it," he told her. "I like the job. I like the people. They money is secondary. Besides, I have that little nest egg." Diya agreed, reluctantly, that the sweepstakes winnings made a difference.

One night as they were eating at a Hooligans' Bistro she said, "All right. It's time to decide. Are we getting married or not?" Diya knew the story of his relationship with his first wife. She promised him that she would not run around with other men or leave him for sex or because she was bored. Because his luck seemed to be changing in other ways, Steve decided that perhaps it was changing in his personal life as well.

Three weeks later, in front of a dozen of his former and her current co-workers from *Abundance*, and a few of his new friends from the food bank, they were wed. The municipal judge who married them Googled Diya's name and discovered it meant lamp or light, and going off the standard book version of quickie city hall vows, he exhorted Diya "to be Steve's light," and Diya to "appreciate the glow of her light as Steve reflected it back." To Steve this seemed sweetly poetic, though Diya confessed to him later that it seemed hokey to her, "something someone who doesn't get a single thing about Indian culture would say."

They went to Trinidad and Tobago for their honeymoon, because Steve read on the Internet that there was a substantial Indian population there and he thought that it might be fun for Diya "to be among her people," a notion she chuckled about but thought was a nice impulse. It was cheaper going to Trinidad than going to India, but when they got there she told him she was not all that interested in the indigenous population or going to shrines, temples, or religious festivals staged for tourists. She wanted to sun herself by the pool or on the beach during the day, and dance at the hotel disco at night. She even got him up on his feet, though he danced like a thirteen-year-old who had just had a growth spurt and was too far from his feet to be sure they would land him steadily on the floor.

In bed on the first night of their honeymoon, after a lobster and shrimp curry dinner at the Indian fusion restaurant by the hotel pool, they had sex for the first time. Once they decided they were going to be married, Diya suggested that they wait until they were legal to consummate their union, and Steve convinced himself that perhaps this made sense. In his first marriage, sex and love had been all confused for him, from the desperate quickies before they were hitched to the infidelities that came at the end. With Diya, he thought, putting things in the right order might make the marriage work better in the long run. While their relationship wasn't traditional in the way that her parents' arranged marriage had been, Steve thought that perhaps Diya's desire to wait for sex was an attempt to honor the traditions of her upbringing. So despite his growing desire for her, and the fact that neither of them was saving their virginity for the other, they waited.

The honeymoon sex was pleasant, if not earth-shaking, and they both fell asleep contented. Over the next six days they made love every night with much the same degree of satisfaction. By the end of the honeymoon Steve felt like they had gotten into a groove. He had come to distrust the explosive bouts of sex he had with his first wife, sometimes crazy as television wrestling matches, with her pinning him to the bed and grinding away on top of him until he was raw and she had collapsed in pleasure or exhaustion, he wasn't always sure which. When he saw that Diya was content with a calmer, less desperate coupling, he was pleased. He began to believe that perhaps she was right, that they would learn to love each other more and more deeply and that this marriage, like her parents' marriage, would last.

Diya did not tolerate living in his tiny apartment for long. It was too small for two, even he had to admit that, and not all that well located, and so they began to seek a new place. They had different ideas about neighborhoods and styles of building. She thought living in the center of the city would be great fun; he thought it would be nice to see some trees and grass out his window, both of which were absent in the view from his current place facing another row of identical structures in the rental development. He had been content to rent all the years of his first marriage. Diya wanted to own, a condo at least. She thought they could get by without a car if they lived near transportation. He loved his new Camry and did not want to give it up. In the end, they moved into a center city high-rise, into a condo, but he kept his car. Some of his newer furniture and his new bed came with them, but most of the furniture came from her apartment. It was an odd mix, but between them they were able to find a set of things that addressed their divergent tastes in comfort and decoration. He had his leather recliner from West Elm, and she a traditional over-stuffed armchair, which she covered with pillows in splashy pastel prints. They brought her sofa and his fifty-inch plasma TV.

As time passed, Steve and Diya adjusted to living together, and made their peace with their differences. They had different diets and different habits. She had grown up eating Indian food, never any beef, and he had grown up a virtual three-meal-a-day meat man. The sweepstakes winnings and their two jobs allowed him to eat what he wanted, and though he would never have described himself as an adventurous eater, Diya persuaded him to get out of his comfort zone and try new foods. Red lentils with spicy yogurt sauces, various piquancy and heats of curry, zalfrasi, and vindaloo, salads with mango, tandoori chicken and fish. She turned out to be an exceptional cook, and her masalas were wonderful. However, if he wanted a steak, she insisted he cook it himself.

Not only at home, but visiting her family, meals were feasts. Though he was mildly embarrassed about his own family of origin, suspicious because of his memory of overbearing and ill-intentioned relatives, he came to love her extended family – a sprawling clan whose pleasure in each other's company was complete and uninhibited. He and Diya visited her transplanted family in Northern New Jersey regularly, aunts, uncles, and cousins. Sometime during his first year of marriage, Steve realized his eczema seemed to have spontaneously nearly completely disappeared.

For their first anniversary they went to see her parents and sisters in Bangalore. He was relieved to discover they all spoke English, at least a little, and he was able to understand if not always participate in their conversations about politics and sports. Because of Diya, who was a rabid soccer fan, he had come to appreciate the game, and had even chosen international teams to follow. Soccer seemed much more interesting to him than baseball or football, which he had never much liked. Her father was also a fan of cricket, a game that Steve simply never fully understood, and seemed interminable and boring to him.

In New Jersey, her uncles and cousins discussed investments and business, and though they did not always remember to include him in their discussions, when they did they asked his opinions and listened respectfully if he had any, which about business matters he mostly did not. And although he was never sure what they thought of it, they always remembered to ask about his work "helping the poor."

Steve had never participated in the high-volume lunchtime arguments his former *Abundance* co-workers had about Obamacare or unions in the workplace, nor was he much more willing to make his views known in the lunchtime discussions his new work friends had about how the Tea Party had ruined the country by hating immigrants and poor people, or how they hated people who only listened to the assholes who bloviated on Fox News. He had never in his life listened to Bill O'Reilly or Rush Limbaugh, and had no desire to. People who had unyielding ideas about what was right about some issue always seemed to be justifying themselves in some uncomfortable way at some later point. For Steve, politics were all about who seemed to be taking care of workers like him. Even though he never listened to him, he knew what Rush Limbaugh stood for, and then he was in the news because he was addicted to pain killers. It was stuff like that that kept him skeptical. He believed in unions, but the management of *Abundance* had effectively kept the United Food and Commercial Workers out of their chain with scare tactics and by strategically promoting rabble-rousers to management jobs. There was a union at the Food Bank, but management was historically so progressive and so completely attuned to giving the folks who worked there the fairest shake they could, that most of what came up was about job-related safety infractions, not salary, benefits, or working conditions. Among Diya's American family, there was a general thankfulness for work, and a sense that many Americans were spoiled and took their country for granted and complained too much when things got hard. Diya stood up for workers' rights to her family, but her father's brothers and their children tended to dismiss her because she was a woman. And because they all worked in family-owned businesses, when she spoke to them about the complexities of the large store workplace and how limiting workers' horizons was tied to making a profit, they were largely blank. The best she could usually do was getting them to agree that workers ought to be treated fairly and well.

After they had been married for just over a year, days after she turned forty, Diya discovered she was pregnant. Both she and Steve were shocked by this turn of events, but decided immediately that they would love to be parents and that they would do a good job of it, even though they were old to be starting a family. Diya knew the risks. She was beyond the ideal age for bearing children, and she was not the most physically fit she had ever been in her life. In fact, she had begun to have slight pain when she walked stairs too fast, and sometimes found herself out of breath when she got through a physical task. Steve ignored the majority of his aches and pains, but he was acutely aware, now that he was married and more physically active than he had been in years, that he needed to pay more attention to his physical health if he was going to raise a kid through infancy, childhood, adolescence, and beyond. But assured that she was healthy by her doctors, and encouraged by her family, who thought her pregnancy was nothing short of a miracle, Diya took to the idea of being a mother with delight, lingering over ads for baby equipment and clothing in magazines and on line. "There is so much cool stuff to buy for kids," she told Steve. "My mother is going to go crazy with this. We'll need to get a bigger place just to store all the stuff she's going to buy."

Steve agreed they might need to move again after the baby was born, that they needed to be looking ahead to questions about schools and safe places for their child to play. His co-workers at the food bank, a mix of folks formerly on welfare and people with Master's Degrees in social work or political science or urban policy, were full of well-meaning advice. They pointed him toward neighborhoods that had great reputations for strong community infrastructure and good schools, and they argued the city vs. suburbs question with each other on his behalf, focusing on schools, public and private, transportation, and lifestyle.

Diya's co-workers, who were also Steve's former co-workers, were also chock-full of opinions, though they tended to be more city-neighborhood focused. After listening to all of their friends, and talking to Diya's family, they decided to stay put in their new place until the baby was a year old. They talked about names and color schemes for the second bedroom, but Diya's family thought it was bad luck to make choices about anything that pre-determined the baby's gender beforehand, and so they made no choices. They had refused the doctor's offer to tell them the sex of their child after the *amnio*.

Steve found thinking about all of the issues of his impending fatherhood daunting. He worried that the bad luck he had experienced in the first nearly forty-five years of his life, everything from his size to his marriage, might transfer to his offspring. Diya did her best to calm his fears. She was pragmatic and tended to discount luck as a factor in anything. She thought perhaps the gods had a hand in some things, and that the reasons things happened were possibly beyond human comprehension. Their discussions of luck ended with Steve saying he only wanted to be a better father than his father had been. "I want to give my child the best upbringing I can," he told her.

"Our child," she reminded him. "Relax."

In her seventh month, at her regular prenatal checkup, the doctor detected an anomaly in Diya's blood work. After a week of tests and a biopsy, and hand-wringing over how the doctors could have missed the change in her breasts earlier, Diya was diagnosed with cancer. Steve was as unready for this as Diya was. He felt as if it was his bad luck coming into play, that the overall course of his luck had shifted again, and that Diya was now the victim because of it. He knew this was slightly irrational, but he could not shake the feeling he was somehow responsible for this turn of events. He vowed to do everything that was important for him to do, and more. In an instant he understood how much he had come to love his wife, and how much he wanted to raise a child with her. If he had felt the pleasure of her company before, the prospect of its loss filled him with a fear and sadness so deep he could hardly stand it.

In the doctor's office, after the diagnosis was confirmed, there was a discussion about the treatment options. Steve sat mute as the doctor described the options – surgery with radiation following delivery, chemotherapy during pregnancy with surgery and radiation afterward if necessary, and surgery plus chemotherapy with radiation during the pregnancy. All three options had risks. In the first case, any delay in treating the cancer meant increasing the risk of metastasis, and although this was the safest overall for the fetus, it posed the most risks for the mother. In the second case, there were some types of chemo that did not endanger the fetus directly, since the placenta acted as a natural barrier to their intrusion into the baby's nutrition. But even these methods could cause issues for the mother, and low birth weight and infections were possible side effects. And there was the danger implicit in delaying the most radical treatments. In the final case, even with highly targeted treatment, the risk of danger to the fetus was high. The doctors gave them twenty-four hours to think about what they wanted to do, and sent them home with pamphlets and lists of web sites they could consult for further information.

They were beside themselves with pain and confusion. After a silent ride home in the Camry, Diya wailed when they got into their apartment. "Will you want me if I am disfigured?" She had started to cry.

"That's what you are worried about? Diya, no. I mean yes. I love you," Steve said, realizing it was true. Diya squeezed his hand. "I will love you no matter what."

"You are such a good man," she said. "It will be all right."

At night, in bed, after they had spent the afternoon reading and re-reading the descriptions of the treatments, the outcomes, and the possible side effects and complications, they decided that surgery now, with radiation following the delivery, was the best approach. Steve had argued for the safest course for Diya, the one with the least risk of harm for her. But Diya reassured him that there was no way she was not going to be around to raise their baby and the baby was all that mattered now. Through all of their conversation, Steve could not hold the thought of Diya's dying in his head, not for the length of their discussion, not in thinking about the future, not at all.

In the waiting room during her surgery, Steve flipped through twenty magazines, all the same ones that had been on offer in the sweepstakes promotion. He could not focus on anything. He thought about whether the sweepstakes had actually been bad luck gussied up as good, if his bad luck had led to this bad turn of events. When the doctor emerged to tell him the results of the surgery he nearly didn't hear them. "A good outcome," he said, "though because of lymph node involvement she has lost more of her left breast than we anticipated. We will talk to her about her options for reconstruction after she has healed, after the baby is born, and we are sure she is cancer free. As of now, we can tell you that mother and baby appear to have come through the surgery fine. You will be able to see her when she wakes up." Steve burst into tears, but he could not say which piece of news was the one that caused him to cry, the fact that she had come through the surgery, the fact that she and the baby were fine, or the fact that she had lost one of her breasts. It was all a jumble, the good and the bad, good luck and bad.

In the days after her surgery, Steve drove directly from work to the hospital, and then after she was discharged immediately home to their place to take care of Diya. He prepared food for her for the next day every evening, and set out her pills and whatever else she needed or requested. The doctors carefully monitored her, and while they took fewer post-operative x-rays than they would have taken if she hadn't been pregnant, they checked her closely to see if there were other signs of tumor growth. They did frequent blood tests and checked her weight and the progress of the baby growing inside of her. A month after her surgery, things looked generally better, and Steve felt he could stop holding his breath. A week before she was due, Diya's mother came from India to stay with them until the baby was born, and while Steve did not relish the intrusion, he understood that Diya was comforted by her mother's presence.

The only thing Steve did for his own pleasure during the weeks between the surgery and the delivery was bowl with the *Abundance* league. His former co-workers were solicitous, concerned about Diya who was on sick leave, and concerned about him. That did not prevent them from busting on him about his impending fatherhood, the same way they had about his marriage. The teasing was just a way to say something, that they were envious; it didn't mean anything bad.

"You'll never have sex on the kitchen table again."

"Kids change everything. Except for the first two years when you change them." Steve even brushed off the veiled implications about the racial mix of his child, cracks about cream in her coffee and *café au lait*-colored kids. He and Diya had never had sex anywhere but their bed, but he secretly liked that his friends from *Abundance* thought that he must have been having wild sex all over the place, although it troubled him a little that they were thinking about him having sex at all. If he had thought about it, he might have wondered if his friends thought that Diya was sexually exotic, capable of doing things their white-bread mates were not. But he did not let himself go there. None of his friends had ever really teased him about his sex life with his first wife, and he wondered if that was because they suspected it was somehow other than normal. It felt to him like the underlying message of their talk now was that whatever he was experiencing in his marriage, they assumed it was pretty much like what they experienced. One way or the other, none of their teasing or the implications of anything they said made him think to ask them to stop.

His co-workers at the food bank saw his marriage completely differently from his old cohorts from *Abundance*. To them, his relationship with Diya confirmed something they believed about people, about what was true about love being blind. They saw his loving a woman of color as proof of human unity, human similarity, and took a certain political pride in knowing them. But it didn't matter to him what anyone thought or said. He knew that even the most foolish comments were well-meant, proof that both his current and his former co-workers felt they could say anything to him, that he was part of each circle's family.

To the players on the *Abundance* league, Steve pretended the pregnancy was difficult but going along generally normally. He didn't want to tell them about Diya's cancer, and she had made it clear she didn't really want people to know. "They'll just want to do things or come around, and I'm not really prepared to deal with that." No one had been told anything about her medical leave except that it was because of the pregnancy. When he was asked about it, he simply said she was having some "complications" and let it go at that.

The baby came two weeks early, but at full weight and healthy. They had already chosen a name, Samitha, Sam for short, and they spoke it with pride to the nurse who was charged with filling out the birth certificate information. "Twenty inches long, six pounds five ounces, and a beautiful head of hair already," the nurse told them. "What does the name mean?"

"It has an Indian meaning," Diya told her, "but we just think it's pretty."

The surgery and eventual radiation treatment did stop the cancer, though they knew they would have to continue to be vigilant. Diya had lost most of her left breast, of course, but it seemed to them a small price to pay. "Amazon Warrior," she said, telling him she had read how Amazon women had cauterized their breasts to more effectively draw back their longbows. In the weeks after the delivery she was too battered to think about reconstruction. And while she tried to hide her breast from Steve as much as she could, he did not find her scar hard to look at or frightening. It was just her now, one part of her was all.

For several weeks after the birth of their daughter, Steve stayed close to home, and close to Diya. No bowling, no late nights at work. His mother-in-law kept Diya company during the day, and prepared a meal for them each evening. At night, after the evening feeding, when Diya drifted back to sleep, after he had cleaned up the Similac fixings and washed the bottle and tossed the plastic liner, he took the baby from Diya and held and burped her, patting her gently on the back. At times, after a few minutes, Diya and Sam seemed to be breathing in rhythm with each other, stereo, one on his shoulder the other next to him on the bed. It was sitting in bed this way that Steve realized that his luck had actually changed, or more precisely that his uneven luck had nothing to do with anything. Things came out the way they did for reasons that were tangled and unclear, but here he was, unaccountably content, in the middle of his life. His wife had paid with a piece of her body for something neither had known for sure they wanted until it happened. He had suffered through his own foolish mistakes, errors in judgment, forces beyond his control. But here he was. Deeply in love. Contented. Lucky.

His cell phone ringing interrupted his reverie. He considered not answering it. He did not want to have to put his baby down and drive to the warehouse to supervise some delivery. Not tonight. But the call was not from work. In the background before anyone spoke he could hear the sound of balls crashing into pins, the pocking sound of the pins falling down. It was one of the guys calling to remind him, in case he had forgotten, that it was Wednesday night, and even though he had missed some of the sessions lately, and his handicap was still for shit, and his crappy play hurt the whole team, they wanted him to know that they still considered him a member in good standing of the *Abundance* league.

PHIL

At Phil's bedside, Zoe felt simultaneously exposed and invisible. Rationally, she knew she was already getting away with the subterfuge. On another level, she could imagine someone, an administrator or a hospital rent-a-cop, or Phil himself, god forbid, finger pointing and declaring *"J'accuse."*

It had been far easier to get into the hospital and into Phil's room than she expected. She simply went to the visitor's check in, mumbled a name and put her hand out. A woman with her own, more permanent name tag that said "I'm Phyllis and I'm a Volunteer!" wrote Phil's room number and 'Natalie Miller' on an adhesive guest pass, then handed it to Zoe without ever looking up. Zoe speculated that the "and I'm a volunteer!" was intended to assure that people would be nice even if Phyllis had to tell them they would have to wait to visit because Nona or Pop-pop's room's quota had been reached. There was an embossed plastic sign on the desk that said "No more than two visitors per patient per room, please." As she walked to the elevators, Zoe peeled the backing off of the name tag and patted it to her blouse, then pulled her sweater half over it so that the edge was visible, establishing her legitimacy but not fully revealing her *nom de guerre.*

Phil was on the eighth floor, the cardiac wing. When Zoe reached Phil's room she stood in the doorway looking in at him. Warren warned her that Phil looked "nothing like the father I remember. After three heart attacks and all the weight loss," Warren confessed to her, "I sometimes don't immediately recognize him. He's that shrunken, that different."

Despite the warning, the visual correlation between father and son was so obscure that she double-checked the room number to be sure she was looking at the right man. Phil was sleeping face up. He had clearly been tucked in tightly by an officious nurse or aide, his sheet drawn up with a hospital crease under his chin. Zoe studied him, but even after several minutes of close scrutiny she could discern not a single feature of Warren's in his father's face. There was nothing to confirm the younger man's genesis from the looks of the older, not facial structure or hair color or skin texture, not the slope of his nose or the line of his jaw.

Though she had not been aware of it, Zoe had inched forward, nearer the end of the bed, and stepped abruptly back, feeling embarrassed – caught – when a nurse's aide breezed in and announced that it was "Time to do Mr. Rosner's vitals. Only take a minute." Zoe nodded, receded further toward the door, pulled her sweater tighter over her, and over the nametag. The aide woke Phil efficiently if not gently, checking her chart and the band on his wrist to confirm a match, then addressing him formally, asked, "Mr. Rosner, what is your date of birth?" Phil rattled it off, this was clearly a routine, and then smiled. Then the aide perched herself on the edge of his bed and leaned in to take his temperature with an electronic thermometer. "Put this under your tongue." She clipped a pulse blood oximeter to his index finger, slid a blood pressure cuff up his arm, and threaded her stethoscope into her ears, multi-tasking effortlessly. Zoe, behind her, was blocked from seeing Phil's face, and knew she was invisible to him. Only when the aide had recorded all the readings on her chart, stowed her gear back in her pockets, and stood to leave, did Phil have a clear view of Zoe. The aide smiled briefly at her as she passed, a smile that acknowledged how sick her loved one was and what a trial it must be to have to worry about him.

When the aide was gone, Phil smiled at her. Caught flatfooted, Zoe asked, "Mr. Rosner?"

"What's left of him." The answer was better natured than she expected it would be.

"Mr. Rosner, my name is Natalie Miller." It was her mother's name, her maiden last name, the same name she had given Phyllis the volunteer at the desk, less likely to forget this than a wholly made up name. "I'm with the social work department," she vamped, "and I'd like to talk to you for a few minutes if you wouldn't mind. The nurses tell me you are quite a talker."

"Really? They talk about me?" It was a guess based on what Warren told her about his father, and she hoped it would overcome any reluctance he might have about her. "I'm flattered."

"We all care about our patients," she said, "and of course we talk about you. You're important to us. Your care is." Zoe felt a small rush of pride at her sudden confidence. She was not a liar by nature, and for that reason had been reluctant to try this when Warren first proposed it. Warren assured her that no other relatives would be visiting Phil, and she would be unlikely to be discovered in her ruse. She talked to her friend Esther, one of her rat pack, who had been a candy striper years ago in high school. "Do they still have them?" Zoe had asked her. "It seems so 1970's." Esther was the only one of her friends who knew about her affair with Warren, and it had been she who suggested the social worker ruse.

"No one will arrest you for impersonating a social worker," she assured Zoe.

Zoe had waited, as Warren had suggested, until the afternoon shift change. "Be in his room a little before four," Warren said. "The outgoing shift won't bother asking you questions and the incoming one will have too much to do to take the time. One way or the other, everyone will assume you're family."

104

Zoe pulled a chair up on the far side of Phil's bed, and angled it so that with only a slight head turn she could see the door. Before she sat, she offered Phil her hand. "I'm sorry to meet you when you are facing such a trial. I invariably wish I had the occasion to know the people I interview before I meet them in the hospital." When she released his hand she sat down, and took a steno pad from her pocketbook and laid it in her lap. It comforted her to have it there, made her feel less exposed, exactly as it did when she laid it on the table in front of her in staff meetings with Warren at work. "Would you mind telling me a little about yourself, Phil?"

"I've given my history so many times I could do it under anesthesia. I will probably have to at some point. They tell me they wake you up just before they cut you to make sure they're sawing on the right guy. I think some hospital somewhere cut off the opposite leg or something. Can you imagine coming in for gall bladder surgery and going home with a permanent limp?" He waited to see if this made her laugh or wince, but she remained steely. "I suppose you want to know about the chest pains and all."

"No. Not really. We know your medical history already. It's in the system. I'm really interested in something else. We're interviewing older patients to get a picture of what their needs really are, or actually, what their needs will be when they leave the hospital after an operation like the one you are facing. What we'd like to know is what your normal life is like? Your medical history is somewhat incidental to our research."

"I wish it was incidental to me." He shifted in the bed, dug his right hand out of the sheet and reached for the bed control, raising himself up so he was almost sitting. Then he pushed the tight sheet down and fiddled with his hospital gown, pulling the top closer around him. "What will come of what I tell you?"

The directness of the question startled Zoe, and she stumbled a little. "Well, with health care reform coming and no one really knowing what that will mean yet," she paused, trying to get her direction, "we're trying to figure out how to allocate resources. We have to be able to tell the insurers what our patients need or they will decide for us. We want to be able to advise the managed care providers and insurance pools what to spend money on." She was cobbling together language she had heard on television from various commentators during the debates over Obama-care.

"I'm a widower. It's coming up on four years. And I'm retired, nearly eleven years now. I spend a lot of time alone in my house. I've lived there nearly thirty years." He looked at her and then looked away, self-conscious for the first time, embarrassed that she might take this for bragging. "Is this what you mean? Is this what you want me to tell you?"

"Yes." There was a pause as she waited for him to go on.

"Are you going to write things down?"

"Probably not most of it. Just my impressions and certain highlights. I'd rather you just talk freely so I can get a sense of who you are. The more you tell me, the more I will know what to recommend."

"I only did one job my whole life." His tone seemed slightly apologetic to Zoe, as if the story of his life was the story of his work life, and therefore essentially dull. "I sold insurance. I worked for a few different companies, but it was really all the same. There were a lot of things I liked about it. I got to meet people, to talk to them about what they needed, sort of like what you're doing. I'm a pretty good listener, and people told me their stories, which I liked. I felt helping them pick insurance was protecting them from disaster, though truthfully, insurance has its limits. Like when disasters actually happen and your clients find out money doesn't really fix the things you most want fixed, or when a kid dies or something like that."

"What do you do now, now that you are retired?"

"A little of this, a little of that. You know. I watch TV; I listen to *All Things Considered.* I read the newspaper. I'm pretty up on current events."

"It's good to stay engaged."

"If it's nice out, I garden. I go downtown to the art museum sometimes. They let people my age in for free. And I can ride SEPTA for free. There are a lot of things like that. The 'pity discount', my friend Lee calls it. You get old, you get pity, that's for sure."

"Do you have many friends?"

"I did. I'm in the process of outliving them. But maybe I'll blow a cold fart on the table tomorrow during the bypass and someone else will win the prize." He raised his eyes to see if she was okay with scatology, and then smiled to show her he wasn't being morbid. "There are a few people I see now and then, old friends from work. Warren, that's my son, thinks if I sold the house and moved into one of those assistance places I'd meet some new people. He's probably right. I just can't bring myself to think about leaving my house." Zoe flinched a little at the mention of Warren's name. She had almost convinced herself that the interview was outside of their world, but his name brought her back to it. "I used to golf and bowl. Now I play cards once in a while, crap bridge and penny-ante poker. A hand of cards is about the maximum I can hold up these days, though they tell me I might progress to a sandwich after the operation."

"Mr. Rosner, are you lonely?"

"Is that on your survey?"

"No. I'm just interested, trying to get a picture...."

"Because there is nothing insurance or Medicare or the new miracle affordable healthcare is going to be able to do to change that."

He waited to see if Zoe was going to respond. When she didn't he said, "If you want the truth, I'm terribly lonely. No one young gives a shit about the old. I got things I could tell them, but everyone knows better. So what are you going to do? Is Obama-care gonna find me friends?"

"Doesn't seem likely, at least not directly. But maybe places where you could meet…."

"Someone wants to pay for something, I could use some physical contact. I don't even mean sex. Just some…" he stopped and shrugged. Zoe felt a little ashamed of herself. "I don't mean it. Not exactly. It would be creepy to have the government pay for companionship. Friends found by bureaucracy? I'd rather be a hermit."

"You're hardly the only one we've heard that from. But what do you think is the solution?"

"Suicide parlors?" He was deadpan. "You know that story? Kurt Vonnegut?"

"I hope you're not serious."

"Yes and no. My life will never be the same. I miss my wife. Even if I found someone else, it'll always feel like a holding action. That's army talk for sticking where you are, not moving forward. In other words, it won't be real life. It'll be waiting with someone. Waiting to die. Which is pretty much what I am doing now. Don't get me wrong, I'm not looking forward to it, but I haven't been pretending since Janet died that this isn't what it is. Now I'm sick. They promise me that after I recover, assuming I survive the operation, I'll feel much better. More active, more inclined to be active, I think the doctor said. Fancy talk. But better for what, I guess is my point. I'm just a little unsure what I am supposed to do. Medicare is spending all this dough to make me better, because Warren and his wife and the grandkids are not ready for me to kick the bucket. And I get that. And there are things I want to live for – graduations and weddings and events like that. But between them, what am I supposed to do with my time?"

"Do you spend a lot of time with your son, Mr. Rosner? Warren? Was that his name?" Zoe was tap dancing now, asking questions she knew the answers to, and beginning to regret the whole enterprise of the interview, of taking Warren up on his desire that his mistress, 'the love of my life' he called her, meet his father.

"Phil. Please call me Phil. Yes, Warren. He and his wife have kids and I see them pretty much every week. They don't live all that far from me. My grandkids like coming to my house because I have a different computer game system than they have at home. They're sweet kids. And I always have junk food. You know, Tastykakes and stuff. "

"I'm sure your son wants you to live a long time so your grandkids can have the pleasure of your company."

Warren's father studied her. "He's a good boy, my Warren. Boy, I call him. He's a man, nearly fifty. To me he'll always be a boy. We have a good relationship I guess, the same as most fathers and sons, close but not friends. I sometimes realize that if we weren't related we wouldn't have any reason…what I mean is, I'm not really part of his life. Not anymore. Not since his mother died. He loves me, he's concerned about me, he's good to me. But it's because I'm his father. You know what I mean?"

"It's like that between a lot of parents and children, don't you think? I'm friendly with my parents, and we care about each other, but we don't share many intimacies. You get beyond a certain age, I don't know, it's hard. I guess I would say I actually lie to my parents quite a bit. By omission, I mean. I don't tell them the whole truth about my life. And the same is probably true for them."

"I am quite sure my son has secrets from me."

There was an awkward silence as Zoe tried to decide if Phil could have possibly intuited her connection to Warren. She felt suddenly muddled, like she was trying to form thoughts in a foreign language she did not know very well. Finally she said, "May I ask you a few more questions?"

"I'm sorry," Phil said. "I've gotten you off track."

"No, no. I just don't want to take up too much of your time."

"Where do you think I have to go? They'll come in with supper on a tray in an hour or so. It'll be lousy. My last supper. Or not. I'll spend an hour eating it like it was a gourmet meal and this was a table at someplace fancy schmancy. I have to be done before eight. Anesthesia. Then I'll watch TV until I nod off. Then tomorrow is the thing."

"Still, I appreciate your taking the time."

"What else do you want to know?"

"Anything else you can tell me about how you spend your time. Do you read? Watch movies?"

"Movies. I have Netflix. Used to like going to the video store to browse. We went from watching whatever was on TV to having all these choices in a store to I don't know, this electric shopping mall. The whole world on your remote. Click and buy. Now, I don't always watch everything all the way through. If they don't catch me in the first ten minutes, I fall asleep."

"What are your favorites?"

"Classics. John Ford westerns. Humphrey Bogart pictures. Black and white pictures no one watches anymore. The Ealing comedies?" Zoe looked at him blankly. "British. Mid-century. Twentieth century." Zoe was blank again. "Alec Guinness? *The Lavender Hill Mob*? *Kind Hearts and Coronets*? *Passport to Pimlico*?" He waited. "Great stuff. Before your time."

Zoe said, "To me Alec Guinness is *Star Wars*. Obi Wan."

"Never seen it. Is it good?"

"It's amazing you haven't. It's a John Ford western in outer space. In color, though. What else?"

"Do I watch?"

"Yes."

Phil lowered his head a little, turned away from her sheepishly before answering. "Hard core."

"Hard core?"

"I hope this doesn't shock you. I like sex films. Pornography. On the Internet. Do you think you can get the Obama-care to pay for that?"

Zoe looked at him for a moment trying to restrain herself and then, unable, laughed out loud. It took her a moment to recover her role. "Mr. Rosner, you are probably the only person I have interviewed who has answered that question honestly. I like you."

He smiled, pleased that she was not shocked. "It's Phil, really. And may I say something in my defense, so you won't judge me too harshly?"

"I am not judging you harshly. Quite the opposite."

"Just the same. I'm not apologizing for this. Just explaining. I like looking at sex since I don't get to do it anymore. I can imagine myself doing those things, the things those actors do. I imagine doing them with my wife. I wish I had had the courage to rent films like these before she died. I'd have learned things. I think once she got over the shock she might have liked watching them, too. She liked sexy books, but she hid them, even from me. She thought she should be embarrassed. Now I've embarrassed myself. I'm talking too much."

"You don't know how refreshing it is."

"My son would crap if he heard me say these things." Zoe did not say anything, and she stilled her face, unsure if Warren's father was right about this or not. Would Warren judge him? "My son thinks he knows me, but you're right we hide things from each other. He is a musician. He has a studio. It's a good business. He's the boss. His clients are all corporate types. I've been there a few times." Zoe had a moment of panic wondering if they had actually met before. Warren had assured her that Phil had not been to the studio in years. She was sure she would have remembered him if they

111

had crossed paths, but what if she had simply not realized who he was or assumed he was a client. She was Warren's general manager. Could she have been working and not realized who he was? Would Phil now put her in that place? Remember that he had noticed her at Warren's studio? Then Phil went on. "My son writes music for commercials. He has staff. He's very successful. I'm sure you've heard his stuff. There's the one about burgers everyone knows, "Our leaner double patties are a quarter less fatty. The bigger burger sandwich at the better burger price." Phil's singing voice was sweet, a reedy tenor like Warren's. For the first time since coming into his room Zoe felt that there was a physical connection between father and son. "There's another one everyone knows, for one of the cell phone companies." He sang half of it, then stopped and waved his hand as if to chase it away. "He's done a lot of them. I can't keep track." The tunes were going around in Zoe's head, and she fought to impulse to admit how well she knew them.

Sitting across from Phil, and disarmed by his honesty, it occurred to Zoe to ask herself what she was doing there, why she had agreed to this subterfuge, in fact why she was conducting an affair with this particular man in this particular way. It seemed adolescent all of the sudden to be the girlfriend of a man who was inaccessible to her in all the conventional ways. At forty-seven, with a bad marriage behind her, it was easy to allow herself to think of what she was doing with Warren as evidence of a failure, a diminishing compromise. But the truth was, Zoe wasn't interested in all the sharing and caring, the dependence, joint ownership and constant deciding that was necessary to keep peace and keep going as half of a couple. If there was only a slim space that social convention allowed for her self-definition – astonishingly, in the middle of the twenty-first century when every other possible kind of relationship existed and seemed sanctioned – and if that definition had the taint of judgment to it, so be it. The other woman, the lady friend, the mistress, the lover, why should it bother her what anyone else thought of it? Or called it? But in that moment, sitting in front of Phil, it did, in part, she knew, because in Phil's world, her relationship with his son was unacceptable, tawdry, threatening. He would believe that in undertaking it, at the very least his son denied his wife something, and perhaps he was right about that. Warren had made the opposite choice from the one she had made; he lived with compromises that she could not bear.

The truth was that Zoe rather liked Warren's wife when they crossed paths. Some days Eleanor breezed into the studio, after a shopping trip, a nearby meeting, or some event with their kids. Zoe felt no jealousy about any of that. Warren and his wife had something separate from what she and he had. And Zoe had friends. She had a real social life and deep friendships, something she had not had during her marriage, women friends. It was Warren who named Zoe's women friends her "rat pack," comparing them to the famous Vegas gang of lounge lizards, Sinatra and Sammy Davis and Peter Lawford, because Zoe and her friends went out on Friday night drinking, and though he was being mildly disparaging and, she assumed, mildly jealous of them, Zoe thought the epithet not wholly inaccurate. They shared a kind of sloppy, jocose verbal intimacy lubricated by martinis, that made Zoe happy, and she often felt most herself, and least guarded, with them. Warren was not a man with "guy" friends, and sometimes Zoe thought the deep loneliness she detected in him, the need that drove him to court her as his lover in fact, would have been offset if he had friendships equivalent to hers.

Despite the fact that they never went home together, she was with him during the day every work day, and enough other times to satisfy herself – at conferences or out-of-town meetings, and occasionally at her place if he could engineer an excuse to stay in town late. She refused to desire or consider more, and she did not miss what she did not have.

113

Until this year, when her daughter went off to college, her own family life had been complex and distracting, with shared custody, and economic conversations about whose half of what had to be taken out of what piece of the pie. She had come to loathe her ex's pettiness about money as much as she had come to loathe almost everything else about him. Theirs was one of those divorces that seemed, to everyone who knew the couple, to come out of the blue, though in retrospect, Zoe knew that was not the case. One day she looked up and realized that she and her husband had nothing in common, that their constant friction about money and possessions was actually about things that were much deeper, and was bad for their daughter. Zoe understood everything that had led to the moment of terrible realization, as she called it: what she had wanted at seventeen when they started dating, and what she thought she was getting – and what she thought she was compromising – when she agreed to marry at twenty-two. But it was all worse than she imagined, the tradeoffs and the losses. Her ex-husband was a professional jock, a wholesale sales rep for a company that manufactured high-end winter sports equipment, skis, boots, and poles, snowboards and helmets, and licensed all the logo-branded gear that completed athletic ensembles. He did not have an artistic bone in his body. She had known this when they were dating, when his desire to have her at his side in exotic ski locations was fun, and more than enough to keep her interested. And she had known it when they married right after she graduated college with her degree in management. He was three years older than she, already started his career, making good money and more of it than he had ever imagined. She thought they would settle in the heart of an east coast city – his company was headquartered in Boston -- and have access to theater and restaurants and ballet – the things she had done from junior high on with her parents, and had come to love. But he wanted to live in Acton so he would be forced to drive his Porsche over thirty miles to work every day. He liked driving, he told her, and if he was going to own an eighty-thousand dollar sports car, he was "damn well going to open it up once in a while."

In the end, everything he did was a calculation, a relation of investment to return. Redo the kitchen? How would it increase the value of the house at sale time? Never mind if it would serve her gourmet impulses. Vacation in Paris? Was Paris a potential market? Could they take the trip and write it off? Would she mind if they went to Barcelona instead, where his company already had a foothold but might be able to do better? Have children? Only one, and no more, for financial reasons.

Suddenly Phil sat up and lurched forward toward her. "I think he wastes his talent. He started out to do something else, something serious, but he got sidetracked." It took Zoe a moment to realize Phil was talking about Warren and not her ex-husband. "I'd never tell him this. He makes good money. He's a great father. But it makes me sad to see it."

Zoe wanted to defend Warren, but she willed herself to silence. "I once wanted to be a writer," Phil said. "I thought if I wrote a book about all the things I thought were wrong with the way people treated each other, it would change things. Pretty naïve, right? Who was I? I had a lousy childhood, like a lot of kids of my era, and if you like calamity stories stop back some time and I'll tell you mine. I'm here all week." He waited for her smile. "Then before I was really out of my childhood, I was in the Army. I had a lousy war experience. This was in Korea, which is another name for hell. It was frightening and degrading. So I wanted to write about it. I even went so far as to rent a little writing studio, well, a room actually, where I went every day at lunch for six months and for an hour at the end of the day. I bought a used Olivetti. No one knew about it, not my wife, not the other guys in my office, not anyone. My little secret. At work they used to razz me about disappearing at lunch all the time. They were sure I had a girl on the side." As he relaxed

115

into his story, he seemed to Zoe to get younger. She could not take her eyes off of him. "I set a goal for myself. Three pages a day. I don't know where I got the idea that was a good number. I must have read it somewhere. Maybe one of Salinger's characters says it. Or maybe I saw it in an interview with Hemingway or James Salter. He wrote about Korea. *The Hunters*. Do you know it?

"Sorry."

"I doubt anyone reads him anymore. The 1950s was a long time ago. The Korean War was not one of this country's best foreign policy initiatives."

She was intrigued by his use of the New York Times reporter word "initiatives," but steered the conversation back to his reading and writing. "I read Hemingway in college. And Salinger. I think people still read them. Undergraduates, at least."

"Well, I thought they were the greatest. 'Course Hemingway killed himself and Salinger stopped writing, whatever that means."

"No one's sure, apparently."

"Well, they were what you aspired to if you were my generation, if you were a man and you wanted to be a writer. Or at least I did. I didn't study it or anything. I just was a reader, an amateur reader, who wanted to write. Anyway, after six months I thought I was finished. I saw an ad in a magazine about getting your book published. I didn't know anything. I didn't know how it was really done, so I sent them the manuscript. They said they'd publish it, but I had to pay. Even that didn't put me off. I figured I could give the book to my friends if nothing else. It would shut the guys in the office up if they could see what I was up to during all those lunches. But by then some time had passed and I re-read what I had. You know what it was?"

It took Zoe a minute to realize he wanted an answer. "What was it?"

116

"It was about three hundred pages of crap. I realized I was kidding myself. I had written a story all right, but it was for me and not for anyone else. I put it away. I never sent them the check. I might have been good, but not writing that way. I would have had to spend years working on it, refining it, rewriting it. I told myself I didn't have it in me. To do that, I would have had to quit my job, maybe quit my family, too. I would have had to be someone else. It was very clear to me. I wanted the life I had more than I wanted that. I wanted my family and my home and the routines of my life. I liked the routine of going to that little room, too. But not as much as the other stuff. I thought about trying to get a job where I could do some writing, but when I really thought about it, I hated that idea. I wasn't going to write insurance manuals or something and call myself a writer. I gave up the room, sold the typewriter. It broke my heart, but it was the right thing. So when I tell you that it makes me sad that my son wastes his talent, I know whereof I speak. I didn't have talent. I might have been able to learn some craft, but nothing I ever wrote would have come naturally. He has talent. Natural talent."

"Maybe he has chosen his family the same as you did." She couldn't believe these words were coming out of her mouth.

"I know. I understand what he's doing. As a result we don't talk about what's important. What could I say? 'Don't sell yourself short?' I watch dirty movies. Who am I to talk?"

*   *   *   *

"How did it go," Warren asked when he got her on the phone that evening. He was on his cell, calling while he was out walking the dog.

"I didn't get caught."

49 SECONDS IN THE BOX

Mira waits in the lobby of her building for the elevator, a canvas bag with an *All Things Considered* logo over her right shoulder. One of her neighbors, Arnie Paul, who has recently moved into the building, steps up beside her. Also waiting is a pair of millennials who live on the third and fourth floors respectively, in condos the owners have rented out. Both have their eyes fixed on their phones, checking messages, texting. The elevator dings. There is a slight pause between the signal that the car has arrived and when the door slides open.

Mira and Arnie start to enter the elevator simultaneously, playing "after you Alfonse" for a moment. Then Mira yields and Arnie goes first. The millennials follow her. Arnie notices that Mira does not have her dog with her. It is the first time Arnie has ever seen her without her Labrador snugged up against her leg. Mira shifts the *All Things Considered* bag from right shoulder to left. The bag holds the leash and collar of the missing dog, Jake. Mira finds her spot, then stares at the floor.

Arnie pushes the button for the seventh floor, the floor on which they both live, she at 706, he at 702. At the last minute, a man with a Roto-Rooter uniform enters. He carries a toolbox and a drain snake. He seems to have come from nowhere. He chunks his toolbox onto the floor, pulls a folded up work order out of his shirt pocket, reads it, and stuffs it back in.

The door of the elevator glides shut. There is a familiar click as the interior and exterior elevator doors disengage. The Roto-Rooter man reaches over and pushes two. Glancing up, Mira notices that the buttons for three, four, and seven are already pushed, but she has not seen that happen.

As soon as the elevator starts to rise, Mira counts under her breath. She is counting backwards from forty-nine. This is the second time she has counted down today. She is coming from the vet's office. The vet has cared for Jake for eleven years, ever since he was a puppy. Dr. "Please call me Steve" Saylor, is solicitous and kind. He sits on the linoleum floor during exams and procedures, getting down on the dog's level, clearly a dog lover.

Mira looks at her shoes, hoping her neighbor does not talk to her. She does not particularly like him and does not want to talk to anyone today. Arnie has made it abundantly clear that he was not a dog lover. Despite this, Mira feels sorry for him. Arnie is the caretaker of his dying wife. Mira sometimes hears her moan when she passes their door on the way to her own apartment.

The five passengers ride in silence. The whir of the motor and the winding sound of the lift cable fill the car. When Mira's daughter comes to visit, she always complains about how long it takes for the elevator to make the climb from the ground to the top floor. "That's five minutes of my life I'll never get back," she says each time to her mother. She has always been prone to exaggeration, though Mira cedes the point about the elevator's speed.

The elevator dings as it stops at the second floor. The door opens. Mira pauses in her countdown. When Mira timed the ride years ago, she pushed start on her wristwatch timer precisely when they started to rise. The trip clocked out at forty-nine seconds. She checked and rechecked it a dozen times. Since then, each time she rides she counts backwards under her breath from forty-nine, finding a kind of meditative purpose in it, her dog at heel, her hand scratching his head. Today, waiting in the vet's office, with Jake lying at her feet, she made a tally. Four outings together a day, times two trips founding partners. The occasional matter he handles tends to require more hand holding of ancient clients than actual knowledge of law. The younger partners handle the legal work now. Though his briefcase is polished leather and looks like it contains items of importance, he is bringing it home empty except for an uneaten apple, a half full bottle of Ensure, and his keys. These are not untypical contents.

Mira shifts the bag from her shoulder to her arms. As she looks inside, a gasp catches audibly in her throat, causing Arnie to make momentary eye contact with her, then look away. She could not explain why she wants to bring Jake's gear home, or what use she could possibly have for it.

At the fourth floor, the elevator dings then stops again. Mira pauses in her counting. The door opens. The other kid gets off. Then the elevator is empty other than Mira and Arnie. They continue to avoid eye contact. The door closes. The elevator starts; Mira resumes counting.

As a child, in Reading, PA, Arnie had lived on the outskirts of town near an immense dairy farm. The farmer had dogs, and their job was to scare off anything that came too close to the cows. Or at least that's how Arnie understood it. In fact, most of the dogs on the dairy farm were herders, used to move cows from pasture to pasture when the grass in one area was eaten down to the nubs, or back to the barn for milking. The farmers and his sons did not treat their dogs like pets, not like the people who lived in Arnie's building now, who dressed their animals with absurd sweat shirts and elaborate collars. Arnie had not liked the farm dogs, and had been chased and bitten as kid, but with distance and age he had come to admire them. They were working animals, he told himself, not substitute children. In his apartment building, even the hipsters cuddled and coddled their pooches as if they were family members, showing them deference and making excuses for them that they would not make for human children if they had any. Even though Arnie recognized that Mira's dog had been better behaved than most of the others in his building, he was purposeless as far as Arnie was concerned, and therefore essentially a resource waster, beneath his contempt.

Jake was the finest dog Mira had ever trained. It was Jake for whom she had coined the term "Box" as a command meaning "enter the elevator." "Box" was part of the simplified, mostly monosyllabic vocabulary she spoke to direct his movement and activities. The single word "Elevator," which Mira could have used as a command, seemed too cumbersome. Inelegant. Inefficient. Mira wanted to be sure that she could always control her dogs with simple verbal instructions. Sit. Wait. Stay. Okay. Leash. Chair. Box.

Arnie knows that Mira has written a best-selling training guide specifically aimed at people who live in tight city apartments with large dogs. The book brought Mira surprise fame and fortune at a time in her life when she would have least expected it. Eleven years ago she had been fifty-six, a refugee from the suburbs, a middle-aged widow living on the proceeds of her husband's life insurance.

The elevator dings as it stops at the fifth floor. The doors open, but there is no one on the elevator getting off and no one on the landing getting on. Mira pauses in her counting, waiting for the door to cycle. It seems to take forever, but finally closes.

She could hardly have guessed when she started work on the dog book that she herself and her best boy, Jake, would become favorites on the local talk show circuit or that her highly responsive but non- trick performing dog would become the model for the great urban house pet. The book had led to classes and workshops, the spreading of her training gospel. But she had also heard her name raised in anger at community meetings where shop keepers and dog hating residents had accused her of "abetting" the large dog influx into center city apartments, with the attendant street-level problems of too much pee and poop. "If Mira

125

Hendricks hadn't written that damned book about how easy it was to keep large dogs in apartments," she heard one of her neighbors fume at one of these meetings, "we wouldn't be doing the sidewalk ballet we do every morning to avoid the dog shit." No one at that meeting seemed to know she was among them, though it was generally known that she lived in the neighborhood. She learned to let these kinds of comments pass. It was the humans, of course, who deserved her neighbors' anger, for not picking up after their pets, but it was the dogs that got banned from buildings and parks as a result.

She wanted Jake to be a good citizen, to live unobtrusively among the humans with whom he shared sidewalks and lifts and hallways. She taught him as a puppy not to jump up on people, not to respond to strangers inviting him over for pets or treats, unless she gave him permission

The command she used to allow Jake to respond to anyone's offer to pet him was "Get love." Arnie had heard Mira say it the one time he had sought to pet Jake, the week after he moved in, a gesture of neighborliness he had no intention of repeating. Labrador Retrievers, the breed Mira had as pets since childhood, responded best to short, clear commands they heard consistently in recognizable situations. In this way Jake had been trained to understand the etiquette of the elevator. At the threshold, on the single command, "sit," he waited until the door opened. He did not lunge when it did. He waited until given permission to enter. On the word "box" he entered and sat, waiting until the doors opened at the destination floor. Once there, Mira said "okay," meaning it was all right to exit. He never pulled her or strained on the leash. Even Arnie noticed this.

The elevator dings as it passes the sixth floor. The leash was never a restraint for Jake, but a signal that an out-of-apartment adventure was about to begin. She used the word "leash" to mean "come and get geared up," to mean "let's go out for our walk." He always came eagerly.

This morning, for the first time ever, calling him to the leash felt like a betrayal. There would be no adventure. There would be no return home. It did not matter that in the last few weeks, when they walked, he would shit out a thin, bloody gruel and then lie down in the snow and close his eyes. Metastasized cancer, clearly dying, but unable to die. It did not matter that he could not tell her in words that she had his permission, or that he signaled he was ready, that he knew his time had come. She knew what he was saying.

Arnie and Mira face in different directions as they ride to their floor. Typically, Mira comes into the elevator with Jake at heel, turns to face forward with the dog by her side. Arnie nearly always rides with his back against the side wall, looking at the other riders in profile, if there are any. Arnie wonders now, in the silence of their ascent, if this choice makes other passengers uncomfortable. Making people uncomfortable is one of the many tactics he has used as an attorney to get the upper hand over his opponents. He has done it so long, and it is so deeply ingrained, that he barely notices that people stand off from him. Looking at Mira opposite him in the elevator car, he is struck by how youthful she looks. Or perhaps it is that, in comparison to his wife, and despite her tears, Mira looks hale and hearty to him.

Nearing their floor the elevator slows. Arnie turns toward the front. When he first moved in, Arnie thought living in a building would prove friendlier than the gated community where he and his wife had lived west of the city, before she became sick, before she could no longer manage. At the ding on the seventh floor, the door opens. Mira rushes out ahead of him, toward her apartment. She does not hear any sounds coming from Arnie's apartment as she passes, and tries not to think about what that silence might mean.

She already has the key in her hand when she reaches her door. Arnie watches her from his door, takes a deep breath, steeling himself to go inside, then suddenly he calls out to Mira, "Are you all right?" "No I am fucking not," Mira wants to shout at him, "and I never will be," but she simply cannot make the words come.

Before the vet gave Jake the injections, when they were all sitting together on the floor of the consultation room, the dog's head in her lap, she leaned into his ear and whispered, "Get love." The dog, nearly too weak to breathe, none-the-less licked her hand. After the first shot of sedatives and the second of barbiturates, Mira counted down to Jake's death. She scratched his head and nuzzled his neck, an act of devotion, waiting for his heart to stop. Forty-nine, forty-eight, forty-seven, forty-six. She knew it was an arbitrary place to start, but it felt right to her, and she desperately wanted him to make it, one last time, to the end. At twenty-four she knew he was gone, but she did not stop counting. Twenty-three, twenty-two, twenty-one. All the way down to zero.

(49 Seconds in the Box was originally published in the Fall 2015 edition of *Philadelphia Stories*.)

DIMINISHMENT

My name is Beverly Anne Fine, and I'm a *crip*. A *quad*, actually. A quadriplegic. Up until the time of my accident, I was called Bee, my childhood nickname, but after my spine was crushed people seemed to think that calling me "Bee Fine" – when I was obviously never going to walk again – was an unpalatable irony. I could have become Bev, but I chose to be Annie – my post-accident identity. Names and categories, you see, matter to me. I have spent considerable time thinking about the language of diminishment and the language of its opposite, what the disabilities world calls empowerment. Handicapped, the polite word for someone like me in the 1970s, always struck me as a prison sentence. *Crip* was the self-designating word that hip gimps started using three decades ago when that supposedly polite word, and its clinical brothers "paraplegic" and "quadriplegic," were rejected as tags by the *para* and *quad* community. I admit I liked the slightly scary if absurdly incongruous associations the word had with the L.A. street gang the Crips, as if I had even the slightest potential for violence, drug dealing, or other gangbanging activities. Some of my wheelchair-bound friends prefer to call themselves *gimps*, another smirking reclamation, but I liked the audacity of *crip* then, and I like it now as a sixty-two-year-old "long-term-injury-survivor." It retains its improbable power to shock.

The story of my accident has lost none of its power over the years, as a source of both anger or sadness for me, though for a short while after it happened, when I was eighteen, it also conferred on me a kind of pitiable specialness, and I told the story with a ghoulish relish to anyone who had the temerity to ask how I had gotten this way. People who wanted to know the story usually took an apologetic approach. "Do you mind?" they'd ask. "How did it happen? I mean, if it's not too hard to talk about." The truth was, talking was all I had, so I answered in high-definition, Technicolor, micro-detail, telling the story with a slightly accusatory directness as if to say, "I dare you, now that you have asked, to try to hurry me along or to turn away or to ask me to soften my tone." I was eighteen, and damaged as I was, what else did I have to distinguish myself?

The accident occurred during my first semester at college. There was some gallows humor I heard from a Vietnam Vet when I was in high school, that if you were going to get killed "in country" you should do it early in your tour so you didn't spend all those months in hell only to get sent there permanently just before you got out of it. Okay, maybe not as blackly comic when it's about a debilitating accident to an early-term college freshman, but you see the irony. I had traveled optimistically cross-country from my home in Indiana, Pennsylvania, the town where the movie actor, Jimmy Stewart, was born and grew up, to Boulder, Colorado, because I believed, from the glossy recruitment brochures that I saw in my guidance counselor's office, that Boulder was beautiful, hip, and arty – everything that Indiana, Pennsylvania was most decidedly not – and it was exactly fifteen hundred and six miles away from my parents' farm, six miles more than the minimum distance I promised myself I'd travel away from my parents and my childhood home.

Early in my first semester I met a boy in the library who, at first glance, embodied all of the attributes I was convinced I wanted in a boyfriend. He had long hair for one thing, what was already being called, somewhat derisively, "hippie-length hair," though I still like it. He had a soulful, Oscar Wilde-like demeanor, and he had been bold enough to intrude on my solitude to ask about the book I was buried in, the novel *The Crying of Lot 49* by Thomas Pynchon, which features an underground postal system, as an alternative to the official one. Pynchon intuited that Americans needed something like it, a way to communicate that bypassed official channels and avoided government snooping into our personal communication or political missives. Of course, now that we know that the National Security Agency listens to everything we say, the joke is on us. But the impulse to have privacy from the government was real then, back in the conspiracy-theory, anti-war seventies, as it is now. In my political naïveté I certainly conflated my need for privacy from my parents' snooping with the paternalism of big government, but if I did I was not alone among my peers in doing so. The government, the establishment, the man, big brother, whatever now-cliché-burdened name we gave it, we believed was the agent of control in exactly the same way our nosy, intrusive, moralistic parents were, and the idea of an end run around them was appealing, or at the very least worthy of conversation with a passionate and soulful boy one might happen to meet in the library. And so it was the small off-campus apartment belonging to this bookish and agreeable boy, Howard Franks from Kansas City, Kansas, from which I was walking home in the very early morning hours of the first week in October, 1970, when I was run down by a motorcyclist and paralyzed.

Howard's apartment was on what was called "University Hill," an area just off the northwestern edge of the campus. I never saw the motorcycle that hit me, or heard it either, until it was too late. I was floating, lost in dreamland. I had just joyously shed my virginity. I had never felt the world more open or more full of possibility than I did during that morning's walk. I felt elated, dirty and cleansed, grounded and airborne, totally off the earth. My new boyfriend, for that is what he surely was at that moment, was still sleeping when I left him, though he had roused himself enough to ask where I was going, and pull me back toward him and utter the single word, "Stay." Was ever there a more romantic word? Nothing he could have said would have served his or love's cause better than that word in that moment.

He had done everything right. Our evening had been perfect, food, wine, marijuana, sex and then this simplest of declarations, his desire to remain entangled with me, all the proof I need of love's palpable magic. Even so, I left him there, drifting dreamily back toward the real world of my straight A, safe-college-rebel-girl, goody-two-shoes life. I had to shower and get my books for an eight o'clock class, though in truth I was considering skipping the shower and leaving his mark and smell on me at least for the rest of that day if not for the rest of my life. You can see how deliriously besotted I was – I think I have even used the phrase "drunk with love" other times I have described my feeling that morning. The small impressions he made in my back and arms with his fingers, the hickey on my thigh, and the funk we made together that I was carrying home with me like the base note of an exotic perfume, even the slight pulsing ache I felt from the rending of that tiny piece of flesh I believed divided my love-life into before and after, these were the badges of my entry into my new grown-up existence, and I wore them with pride. Any pain I felt in the shock of his entry into me, any embarrassment about the slight stain of blood I left on his sheets after the fact, was overwhelmed by the feelings of pleasure and joy I had in accomplishing this seduction and surrender. It was, exactly, how I imagined a first time, painful enough to be memorable, pleasurable enough to suggest the pleasures to come.

Before I left, I kissed Howard back into his dreams and fairly skipped out the door, having discarded the last vestige of some code of honor that I felt had been presented to me at puberty which I had then worn like an amulet through high school, assuming that to break it would be my ruination. I know there were other places in America by then where these Victorian notions of sexual self-preservation, saving one's self for marriage or at least for verifiable "true" love – if verification is ever possible – or saving one's self for any other reason, had disappeared into the smoke of what my parents called "the fires of social permissiveness," but in the provincial town where I grew up they had not. Small towns impose their moral codes by proximity and gossip.

Indiana, Pennsylvania was a very small, very imposing town, more churches than bars, more cows than people. While the University that is now the major employer in the region had begun to expand, farming was still the work of choice in the county. Town, with its two traffic lights two blocks apart, was where you went for groceries, livestock feed, and hardware. (Jimmy Stewart's family owned Indiana's only hardware store.) I knew that there were no boys anywhere in the proximity of that town or near my age with whom the pursuit of physical pleasure would have been worth the resulting ostracization. But in Boulder, I was certain, there would be boys who interested me, and in giving myself to them I would incur little or no risk of social or moral judgment. When I received the application brochure in the mail, with its cover photo of serious kids walking through the campus in serious conversation, in their patched jeans and long hair, I knew I had to go there. I was the only person in my high school class who applied to go to a college significantly beyond the nearby city of Pittsburgh or the few hour drive to Philadelphia. A few went south, to Maryland, some to Penn State in Happy Valley. But most stayed in town and went to Indiana University of Pennsylvania, a name which, other than in Indiana, Pennsylvania, itself, never failed to raise an eyebrow.

"Indiana University of where?" my girlfriend Lisa and I would say to each other during our senior year of high school, while we were plotting our getaways. "Indiana middle of nowhere, that's where," the other would respond.

133

For me, leaving was an imperative. I did not want to be able to be called home on weekends. I did not want to worry about ever running into anyone who knew me, my foolish aunts or practical uncles, my father's Grange buddies, or volunteer fireman acquaintances. I never wanted to have to reckon with the difference between whatever I chose to be in the present and any past versions of my all-too-good-girl self.

I had started to practice for college the summer before I went. I knew I wanted to smoke marijuana, and so I methodically learned to smoke cigarettes, hiding them from my parents, of course, teaching myself to inhale so I would have the capacity to hold the smoke deep in my lungs for extended periods when the fat joints I imagined would be passed around at parties were passed to me. There were kids who smoked grass in my high school, but they were not in my circle, to the extent that I even had a circle. I didn't like most of the people I went to high school with, content with themselves as they were, content with their sleepy, self-satisfied town, with the status quo in all things. Whatever defiance or non-conformist habits they cultivated in high school, and from this distance looking back I realize that some of my classmates must have cultivated them, they hid them behind the facade of indifference, not wanting to stand out in any way in that judgmental and narrow place, just as I hid my dreams of a richer, hipper, more cultured, more sensuous, and more fulfilling life. I wanted all of my experiences to be high-minded and passionate and deeply meaningful. As I say this now, I think with shame on the amount of time I have spent over the last forty years watching awful TV, making time simply pass without meaning, avoiding the implications of my limitations.

It is probably fortunate that the boy who ran me down on his two-year-old 1968 Triumph Bonneville 650cc Motorcycle, model T120R – I remember the details precisely since they so came to define me – came from a family that

134

had both money and conscience. They believed in the necessity of taking responsibility for their son's actions.

My motorized assailant's name was Paul Boyer. His father owned a large cattle ranch west of Boulder. Paul had learned to ride motorized dirt bikes as a rancher's son, on a spread where motorized dirt bikes had replaced horses as the means of moving stock from one pasture to another. Old Paint turned into rolling thunder. Like me, Paul had been heading to his own apartment from the apartment of a lover, going home to get ready for school, and sleepy or stoned or simply not expecting to encounter anyone that early in the morning. It was six thirteen AM. He was moving too fast downhill to have stopped in time. Proximate causes, like residual sexual bliss or marijuana or alcohol inebriation, or plain old tiredness, or a hundred other possibly relevant explanations aside, our collision was simply an accident. Paul laid his bike down on its side trying to avoid me, exactly as he had been taught by his safety-conscious father, but his legs, dragged along the asphalt by the bike's momentum, clipped my ankles and knocked me off my feet. I was upended, flipped upside-down in the air. In the moment between the impact of his skidding body on my ankles, and the impact of my body on the street, I saw myself as if from above, doing a kind of slow motion pirouette. In my mind, I saw the triangulation between the apogee of my flight and the ground, and I knew I was going to hit badly. When I tell people I saw this in my head while I was still in the air, they tend to nod indulgently. "Sure she did." But the geometry of my tragedy was perfectly clear to me in that moment; I knew while I was still in the air what was coming, and no air swimming was going to prevent it. I landed on my neck, and came to consciousness on the asphalt with no feeling in my torso, arms, or legs.

The only thing I could think of lying there was that it was just my luck that the one absurd piece of advice my mother gave me repeatedly as a child, that embarrassed me every time she offered it, came back to me at that moment. My underwear was not clean. It was, in fact, filled with the proof of what my mother would surely have called "my sinful behavior." "What," she had asked me often back in my childhood, "would you do if you suddenly had to be taken to the hospital and your underpants were foul?" Besmeared with the fluid evidence of my night's activities, the scarlet and chalk evidence of my transgression would most certainly be seen by the emergency room doctors and nurses whose knowing if silent judgment I would forever internalize. Lying there, I knew one other thing with blazing certainty, though no diagnosis of my future mobility had yet been made. I knew that my sex life was likely to be forever over, punishment for what my mother would have called my recklessness. I was sure I would never know such pleasure or happiness again as I had, just hours before, experienced with Howard. It was this thought that made me cry, not physical pain, which I was not feeling, though the emergency medical technician treating me assumed the opposite and gave me a shot of Demerol.

I remember nothing of what followed – being strapped to the back-board, being transported by ambulance to the hospital, being x-rayed, having my scrapes and bruises dressed, having my reflexes and responses tested and retested. Everything I know about my post-accident emergency treatment is second hand, from information my nurses and doctors and members of my family reported to me afterwards, and from official descriptions the police wrote down in their reports and the insurance companies included in their investigation. I have tried many times over the years to force myself to remember more, because after being airborne, after hitting the ground, everything slipped off of one track and on to another. It is into that gap that I have placed all of my losses, all of the changes between before and after. Without first-hand knowledge of those moments between landing and passing out, between triage and treatment, I have always felt totally liberated to tell my story to the curious with whatever embellishments I deemed gory or visceral enough for the listeners to digest, for whatever quotient of pity or sympathy I wanted to wring from them, or whatever amount of supposed inspiration for my so-called survivor bravery I wanted to embody.

In the end, after weeks of recovery, as hope evaporated that some miracle would occur, I was left completely paralyzed from the chest down. I had no feeling in my extremities or limbs, no sensation in my torso, no tingling or throbbing or phantom pain. I was simply a log from my armpits to my toes. All I had was the ability to wiggle the fingers on my right hand. I learned to press forward on my wrists, but I could not raise my arms.

Over the years I have come to know a lot of quads. Because I have this little bit of finger flexion, relatively speaking, I have it easy. There was a lot less hope for spinal cord compression injuries in 1970 than there is now, a lot less equipment to make life manageable, too. When I came out of the hospital, after the insurance settlements and the lawsuits and the subrogation, after breaking my mother's heart and convincing my father that the accident had addled my brain by telling my parents that there was no way in hell I was going back with them to Indiana, Pennsylvania to live, with the help of several sympathetic social workers from the hospital, I found myself an apartment and an aide whose job it was to get me out of bed in the morning and clean me up for the day – I had lost control of my most basic functions, you see. With help I learned to find my way in the world. Those were the days when insurance companies stinted less on things like physical therapy and what we now call accommodations, though there was less to stint on. In time, insurance bought me an electric wheel chair I could manage to steer with my fingers and wrists once I was gotten into it.

The University was somewhat accommodating as well, likely more because they were afraid of litigation than

remarks, how sorry he was, how of course he and his family would take full financial responsibility, how if he could take the moment back he would, how he would give anything to have not been driving so fast, he simply stood at the foot of my bed and wept. He was so abject, so wretched, that it took me a moment to realize that he had made no excuses at all, no 'I couldn't imagine anyone would be out at that time of morning,' no 'it would not have happened if I had not been walking in the street,' no 'it was barely light and I was wearing dark clothing.' Nothing. He had taken it on, and for that I was instantly and profoundly grateful. He asked, and then promised he would when I said yes, if he could return "maybe to just sit with you for a while."

It was more than Howard, my hard crush, my library pickup, my one-shot lover, my first friend with benefits as they now say – you see I still have a hard time categorizing him after all this time – had done. Howard, the taker of my virginity, had come as soon as he heard, on the first day of my hospitalization. He was appropriately devastated. How could this have happened? When I looked up at him from my bed in the intensive care wing, I was seeing him from precisely the same angle I had last seen him standing the night before, when our bodies had finally detached from each other. He had stood over me, surveying me in the tangle of bedclothes, and smiled down, loving me in that moment, I am sure, for who I was and what I had given up, and for what we had done together. Looking at me then, he was so clearly contented that he re-energized my own sexual delight, causing the last faint wave of electric pleasure, a reverberating echo of the physical joy I had just experienced, to emanate from between my legs, the last sensation of that kind I can fully recall. In the hospital room, forced by the monitoring equipment and the curve of the curtains that separated me from my equally battered roommate – another car accident victim – my first lover stood in the same position relative to me that he had occupied in his bedroom looking down on the post-coital me the night before.

At the time of Howard's first visit, hours after the shot of Demerol on the street had knocked me out, no one knew if I would or could ever walk again. Hopefulness was the pose everyone struck. The doctors were saying little, refusing to answer even my questions about my future, urging caution and watchfulness, waiting to see how things went, what the tests showed, how my body healed. Blanketed up to my chin, my body straightened under the covers, I suppose I looked pretty much like I had looked the night before, right before Howard had climbed back into bed with me after our love-making, after waiting like a gentleman for me to use the bathroom, when he had paused, standing next to the bed and looked down at me. Was that look gratitude, or love, or pride of conquest? I do not know. He had leaned down and kissed me then, and did so again when he came to see me in the hospital, ignoring the deepening blackness around my eyes. From where he stood could he have possibly imagined that I was the same as I had been when he saw me last? Or was it in that moment that he knew he would not be able to bear spending time with me?

He came back only twice in the two weeks after that, and for a total of twenty-two breezy minutes by the oversized clock facing my bed. He was, I came quickly to realize, without the ability to deal with anything like my injuries, despite his soulful looks and his empathetic style, and so he wouldn't. Whatever we were headed toward had been permanently derailed. I did not blame him. I simply hated him. Not immediately, but eventually. And with him, the world divided into those who had a way of incorporating me into some version of their reality and those who did not. It did not even take weeks for him to be gone from my life entirely.

By the time I had recovered enough to leave the hospital for a rehab facility, and then forced my way through therapy, learned to calibrate my eating and elimination, and returned to taking classes at the reduced rate of two a semester, Howard was gone from the college and gone from Boulder, or so I heard through the grapevine from his friends – the one or two who stopped and spoke to me as I tooled around on campus in my clunky motorized chair. Fearing, perhaps, that he would run into me and have to explain himself, or simply unable to face me, he disappeared, and with him the only witness to my only mutual sexual experience, my one and only accompanied orgasm. Gone, gone, gone.

But I do not want you to pity me for that loss. Up until now, I have had a semi-decent time of it, and my relationship with Paul Boyer was the reason. He remained my friend and confidant for all these years, despite having been my assailant. I think at the simplest level, in the beginning, I was the only person he could talk to about what had happened, about his guilt, or about his feeling that fate had intervened in his life in a trajectory-altering way. As I said, he did not make excuses, but that did not keep him from trying to see things clearly, from having real feelings about the difference between what was and what might have been, for him and for me, both the good and the bad of that. Would we have even known each other if not for the accident? Unlikely, it seems to me. What started out as an obligatory gesture from a decent guy trying to expiate his guilt, and because I was not horrified by his attempt to make such a gesture, became, during my recovery and after, a deep friendship and eventually a love affair, if to all the world a seemingly chaste one. Over the years, separate and aside from his marriage and parenting two children, or perhaps in addition to it, he shared his feelings with me, his secrets, his joys, and his doubts. I have met his wife, Mindy, a few times, a lovely person herself, and someone I believe is quite his equal in character, though I cannot say I really know her, other than what Paul has revealed to me about her. She knew

Paul came to see me and she knew how we met, but if she suspected that I was in love with her husband, or he with me, she was relieved of the burden of jealousy because of how she read my condition, believing that there was no potential for any kind of intimate relationship between us. It was that belief that allowed us to have one. Although by all conventional standards, the physical nature of our love affair was completely one sided, and by some reckonings could be seen, I suppose, as a kind of bizarre exploitation on the part of a fully abled man of a nearly fully disabled woman, like many things involving the human heart and physical desire, it was far more complicated than that.

The details of how it started are mundane. As part of my therapeutic regime, others exercised me on a daily basis, meaning I was stretched and bent and folded and massaged. I was also bathed and dressed to a large extent by aides and nurses and therapists from the moment of the accident on. Any lingering ideas of modesty quickly dissolve under these conditions. Imagine not having the ability to bathe yourself for over forty years? One part of my daily routine was the 'anointing of my body with oil' as King James translated it, the application of lotion meant to keep my skin supple. Over the time he spent visiting me, Paul had seen many of these ablutions administered to me. At first, he removed himself from my room when the therapist warmed the bottles, shamed, I believe, by what their necessity demonstrated, that I was and forever would be in some way dependent on others for the simplest activities, and that he had been the cause. After some time however, he began to be less uncomfortable and if it was simply his inertia or if I actually invited him to stay in the room during one of these treatments, I do not remember. Was the visiting home health aide shocked or simply accepting? I do not remember that either. Whatever her reactions, she must have done this a thousand times in front of reluctant boyfriends before. At some point there stopped being even the vestige of embarrassment, no line of

143

intimacy we felt we were unable to cross. He started rubbing my back and legs with lotion during his visits, and then eventually he took what my mother would have railed against as "scandalous liberties." For me, with sensation as absent as a truant schoolchild, the initial shock of his presumption departed with any traces of embarrassment I might have had about being physically exposed in front of him. What could it possibly matter? If I justified what some might consider my transgression against his wife by allowing myself to be caressed, by knowing I would never reveal our activities, I also felt no moral restraint. I accepted what he offered in the spirit it was offered. And I confess that it gave me pleasure. Not the normal physical pleasure the stimulation of breasts and thighs reliably offers to the healthy, but visual and auditory pleasure – watching him explore my flesh as if it were alive as his own. It gave me physical pleasure to watch Paul do what he did to me, the chaste massages at first, then more and more undressed, and more and more intimate. I watched him take his time with my body, make a kind of love to it, caress it and embrace it limb by limb, feature by feature, fold by fold, opening by opening. And if I felt nothing physical when he eventually slid his fingers and more into me, if my nerves did not fire the flashes of joy I experienced that one time, long ago, or I have since seen woman in pornographic movies enact, or have read about with delight in novels, I did experience the purity of delight on his face as he explored me. If I could not arouse when he rubbed first my breasts and later my clitoris, if I could not orgasm, I could watch him as he gave himself pleasure on my body and thereby partake in his ecstasy and joy.

The one act of love I could perform in a somewhat normal fashion was taking him in my mouth. Even this, though I had partial mobility in my neck and could use my tongue, was not conventional. I could not go down on him in the way that graphic colloquialism suggests it usually happens, woman on her knees bending over a supine man.

144

Or on her knees with her face leaned into him at the juncture of his legs. Without the ability to support myself, with no muscle control of spine, arms, thighs, knees, or feet, I could only imagine myself gagging to death on his erect penis because I could not raise or retract my head. Oral love was an engineering project like everything else in my life, from lifting me out of bed into my wheelchair, to getting dressed, to using the bathroom, to taking a bath. He would move me to the edge of the bed, turn me onto my side, and find my mouth at a height that was satisfactory to him by spreading his legs and bending his knees. He never pushed himself into me beyond the distance he believed I could easily retract, and he allowed me to take control of him with my lips and tongue. When he came, and it was eons before he let himself come in my mouth, despite my assurances that it would be fine with me and even that I desired it, tasting him and seeing his face transformed by orgasm was as great a pleasure for me as the transformation itself was for him. In this one small way I felt whole, I felt normal; I could forget, for a moment, how damaged I was below the chin.

I knew, and have always known, that by any conventional evaluation, what Paul was doing with me – I will not encourage conventional judgment by saying 'to' me – could be considered advantage taking, even a deep perversity, "a sick perversion," I once heard a misguided lecturer on sex and the disabled call it. A fully able man using a flattened, disabled woman as a tool for what amounted to self-stimulation, an accompanied masturbation, an onanism with company. But it did not seem that to me. For me, it was simply the best I was likely to do giving another pleasure, which is, I aver, half the intention of physical love.

Paul made no promises of fidelity to me, and yet was faithful as a man ever was. In the early days, before computers made communication with people like me easier, he called and visited regularly, once a week or so. Later, when there was email, and mobile devices outfitted for immobile quads, we chatted nearly every day. I had early versions of voice recognition software in the late 1980's, and then more and more capable commercial versions. Paul was not the man of letters I once imagined for my partner, not even the intellectual equal of the boy who had waltzed me out of the library and into his bed for my one true fuck, with its disastrous aftermath. Paul was direct and practical in his communication, concerned and chatty. He read newspapers every day; there were several serving the front range of the Rocky Mountain west in those days. He watched Jim Lehrer on PBS and listened to NPR on the radio in his truck on the long drives he often had to take to electrical trouble spots as a supervising lineman for the Boulder County power company. He kept up on current events and politics, told me his opinions, and when he visited, recounted to me the events of the city's and nation's and world's day as he told me the details of his own. We argued and debated. I was generally more liberal than he was, though he often surprised me. He was a willing and open-minded conversationalist, and a good listener who, in his steady-if-unpoetic way, never treated me as a required chore or a needy child or an obligation he had to fulfill, never condescended, never patronized me on the basis of his relative engagement with the world versus my limited one.

Between Paul's letters and emails and his attention to my wrecked body, I have come to believe I could not have had a better life partner. That he lived with another woman, made conventional (and I believe attentive and authentic) love to her, bore children on her and raised them lovingly, supported his family with his labor, vacationed with them, visited his in-laws and later his grown children in far-flung places, in fact tended to his wife and family in sickness and in health, was beside the point for me. Mistress without the ability to seduce, lover without the power to caress, in fact without any means whatsoever for participating in his life unless he chose to come to me, I was nonetheless fulfilled beyond the best compensationalist dreams I had allowed myself to entertain in the weeks and months after he had run me down. I was, I confess, despite the confines of my physicality, often happy.

Imagine how crushing it was then, to learn that Paul had been electrocuted. I have seen pictures of him up in the air in his bucket, selfies he took to show me what he did on the job, or of some vista he was able to see that those of us who were ground-bound, let alone bed-bound, would never see. I do not know the exact spot on Highway 119 in Boulder Canyon where it happened, nor did I even remember the midday rain I gather was falling that day. All I knew was that he and his crew had been replacing the electric poles and lines that ran between Boulder and Nederland that had been compromised by the flood in the canyon in September.

As there never are in accidental deaths, no warning presaged Paul's sudden departure from my life. It was so wrenching, so destabilizing, that I could neither work nor eat for days after I received the news. His wife called me on the day it happened, a wreck herself, barely able to speak. We cried on the phone together. "I know how much he thought of you," she repeated to me several times. I wondered if she was avoiding saying, "how much he thought about you." I believe she knew nothing of the details of our relationship, or about our bedroom activities, if you want to call behavior as physically one-sided as ours "activity." But she was not stupid, and she was not blind, and she knew – and I knew she knew – in her heart that ours was more than a casual friendship, if she disbelieved it could be a love affair. As hard as it was to not express a lover's grief, how could I not comfort her, as graceful as she had been about sharing her husband? What she knew or guessed or intuited – or more likely intentionally ignored – about what Paul did when he came to see me, whatever unhappiness or doubt it caused her, she never once, in thirty-seven years of marriage to him,

147

expressed it. She did not seek to impose any restriction on our time or togetherness, nor impose herself on us in any way. What more evidence of her grace could I have required?

We cried together on the phone, and then she asked if there were things she could do for me that Paul had done, shopping or other things. I was momentarily breathless. I hardly knew how to respond. Did I want her in my life? Could I transpose his eager connection to me into a sense of obligation for her, simply because she had been married to him? Was her offer made impulsively or thoughtfully, because she needed a distraction, or a charity, or something to connect her to something important to him? I did not know.

I told her that he didn't do all that much that was practical for me, other than, while at my house, preparing tea or a snack. How could I tell her that he had sponge-bathed me after our lovemaking – and do not blanch at that word, please, since that is how I saw it – and held me in his arms? We were suffering, in fact, the same loss, grieving the same man, whose goodness or duplicity – whichever way you want to think about it – we shared. In the aftermath of his life, we were both bereft, and the cause was the same. I understand that what he kept secret from her – what we both kept secret – opens us to a harsh judgment. Nor do I fail to see that in some conventional sense I was her rival and that his attention to me robbed her of something – time if nothing else – and some measure of his non-infinite love. But I also wondered, dark as it was of me to wonder it, if she had not also gained something in this as well, some iota of attentiveness he might not have exhibited had he not needed to be as mindful of her because of me. Whatever else one might say about his relationship with me, it did not cause him to stint on his attention, his affection, or his love for her. At his death, we were sisters in grief, though we could share only the simple fact of it. That I understood more than she did about our relationship, hers and mine, changed nothing. Our tears for him were drawn from wells of equal depth.

When I returned to work a week after his funeral – my co-workers had simply been told I was home sick; how could I share my grief with them? – I used my access to legal search engines to find out everything I could about bucket truck safety. I knew from our conversations, that Paul worked with a regular crew of linemen, that he had been the boss on his crew for fourteen years, and that he had refused his employer's repeated offers to take an office job, accept softer work out of the weather, to allow a promotion in recognition of his years of solid and loyal performance. "Taking the arm up" as he called it, suited him, and also satisfied him in a deep way. He like being in the air, liked that he could repair something so vital as the river of electricity that delivered what he called "juice" to people who consumed it, to run their well pumps and lights and heaters and stoves and computers and stereos and mobile device chargers.

I learned that most bucket truck accidents happened because operators themselves take shortcuts with safety precautions. I told myself, when I started researching, that my interest was purely academic, just another facet of my interest in him. There were no reasonable legal avenues of redress for me, as robbed as I felt. Workers compensation and his life insurance policy would pay their benefits to his family regardless of fault. But I wanted to understand something that seemed to elude me, some truth about how a man as careful about everything as Paul had been could have died in this way. I studied the accident statistics and the incident reports, and the number and kinds of regulatory changes that arose in the aftermath of these accidents. I studied everything I could get my non-functioning hands on, realizing that I had not ever made a deep attempt to understand what it was that Paul had done in his work life, even though it was that work life that steadied him, gave him

149

a kind of starting point for the purposeful care he had taken of me. It comforted me to be doing something methodical, something that continued to connect me to him, even if that connection reminded me again and again of the horrible way he had been taken from me. I exhausted myself with OSHA findings, truck and lift-arm accident investigation reports, everything there was to read about the legal actions that had been taken against companies whose workers had had accidents.

I had basically come to an end of that research when it came to light as part of the insurance investigation that Paul's co-worker on the truck may have improperly set a lock meant to keep the bucket from swaying, so that when Paul leaned toward the wires, instead of being secured, the bucket followed his weight, causing his body to "encounter the hot line," in the language of the report, though I cannot put out of my mind the way his limbs must have shaken in spasm as the current coursed through him. Under questioning, this man, Daniel "Hilly" Hillson, claimed that he could not remember what happened before Paul was shocked, and that afterward he was panicked getting Paul down from the bucket, performing CPR, and waiting for the medics to arrive. This part I understand, at least, losing the memory of a terrifying event is how we defend ourselves against shutting down when we need to function through a crisis. According to the police and the insurance report, Hillson did the right things after Paul encountered the wire, performing as he had been trained, trying to restart a dying man's heart. An unpalatable irony in *this* story is that it was Paul's responsibility to certify safety training and accident-readiness for the company. He had trained Hillson in CPR.

After the fact, Hillson told the inquest that he believed he had set the lock as he did every other time an arm went up, but he could not be sure, his memory of the day was muddled – "fried" was the word he used – and fragmentary. He was devastated by Paul's death, suffering terrible guilt

150

and debilitating grief, but what else to conclude than that he had killed my lover? It had been Hillson's job to set the lock; that much he knew. There had been a discussion with Paul about it before he climbed into the bucket. But the lock was not set which, in the clinical words of the report, "caused the situation to exist that resulted in Paul Boyer's death." Beyond that, there was no assessment of blame, no sanction, no punishment. It was deemed an accident. End of story.

My first reaction to discovering this was rage. I, who must be so careful with myself, so controlled so as to be able to survive the day, could barely understand how someone with all of his faculties could be so careless. I concocted fantasies to avenge Paul's disappearance from my life, swift and terrifying and biblical, the way he had been taken from me. I thought about what I would say to Hillson if I ever crossed paths with him, what I would say if I could bolt him to a chair and suffer him to listen to my life's story. These thoughts are all the power available to the powerless, a useless churning. But I let them churn, and images of Hillson's writhing torture comforted me the way executions were once thought to comfort the families of homicide victims. For a while I did not allow myself any psychic real estate on which to gain a foothold of rationality. I did not want to intercede on these black thoughts. I let Hillson suffer in my imagination like a slow boiling sinner in a Boschian hell.

Until it occurred to me to wonder what Paul would do in my place, to think about the fact that I was in a position somewhat parallel to the one I had been forty years earlier, when Paul came to me, abject for his part in my disembodiment, and then stayed to become my lover.

Does analogy of circumstance encourage understanding? Without Paul there was no one to ask. Did Paul's example obligate me to something? To anything? Or was this loss beyond my ability to forgive, given my age and stage of life? Widow who was never wife, chair bound cripple whose airborne heart had been smashed to earth.

As Paul came back into focus for me, as the reality of his loss began to redefine my days, the absence of joy, of anticipation, of love, of everything good and healing and important in my world, I began to think about what had driven him to visit me, what it meant to me, and how I had come to forgive him for having taken what should have been my dance of life and turned it into a crawl. Paul took my escape from the emotional poverty of my childhood, took my stature and my stride, my dignity and my dreams. He took my life as I imagined it and made it lesser. But I forgave him because he gave me something in exchange, not what I imagined or desired or planned for my life, but ultimately, perhaps, everything I could have wanted. He gave me love. He loved me despite having caused the wreck of my body, no – separate and aside from having caused it – not out of shame or pity, but the way love always arrives, unbidden, without reason. And I forgave him, because of that love. It made me feel singular to be able to forgive him, to rise above everything that should have kept me from that. Despite my monstrously damaged body, I was human. That realization saved me from despair. I could forgive. Therefore, I could thrive. I did not want my life consumed with hating Paul. When he came to me, right after it happened, I was a kid, with my whole life in front of me. I was never going to walk, and I knew that my life was going to be hard, and I wasn't going to feel certain things. I know now, and I knew in time, that I may have missed less than I thought I would.

But I am nearly out of time now. This time, I have lost the person I forgave, the person I loved and Daniel Hillson is the cause of it, and I have no will to forgive him, cannot forgive him, because he has made me face the fact that in the aftermath of Paul's death, I am less. He has made me less. Simply less. Diminished. Where I wasn't one before, now I am a crip in my heart. Taking my love, more than taking my youth, my dreams, my mobility, my freedom, he has also taken all the evidence that I am human. He has killed me as surely as he killed Paul, the dual effect of a single act. I forgave the man who cost me the life I thought I would have. But I cannot forgive the man who has taken my love. And because I cannot forgive, I am no longer the person I was. This is the core of my diminishment. When I look into the mirror I see I am another person now.

This, then, is my verdict, for the murder of my love. This is what I want to punish him for, what he must perform penance for. Not only as retribution for the dead, who suffer no more, but for the living as well, where life and hope's been wrecked. I want him to carry his guilt for this, to drag it with him like I do the non-working husk of a body, which is all he has left me of myself.

How We Failed To Stop The War And Other Consequences Of The Adolphus, Alaska, Peace March, February 2003

There were fifty-one of us who witnessed Mac Reedman's heart attack. We were on a peace march. It was cold. Not bone-chilling like it can get here when the temperature hangs at minus ten for weeks at a time like it has some winters, but cold enough that everyone was layered up. Cold enough that my feet took more than an hour to recover sensation after the march, even though I was wearing a pair of thermals under my merino woolies, and I had my insulated Vasque boots on. I know how long it took because I worked on trying to warm them the entire time we waited at Leon's to hear that Ruhl, Daniel, and Mac hadn't crashed into the Chilkats or the Lynn Canal on their flight to Juneau.

The bite the day of the march was because of wind, which was from the west, steady, and heavy with humidity. Sea breezes are our mixed blessing, the reason we don't usually get crushing cold, and the reason it rains here right along the shore more than snows. Because of where Adolphus sits on the coast, once the sun is up, things warm up fast. Sun hits us in town most of the day. Other places on the coast, places in deeper coves than ours, fight mountain shadows, sometimes in two directions as the sun moves. We're in the clear and warmer, if just slightly, than even a mile inland.

The morning of the march the temperature stalled just above freezing. It had rained on and off since sunrise, and everything – streets, cars, buildings – was coated with a liquid slick. Though the mountains to the east were astonishingly white, the only visible snow in town was week-old mounds in places shaded from the sun, or strips clinging to the north side of the scrub pines in that treacle-y sugar-frosted, Christmas card way.

To folks who don't live here, it's always a little mysterious how events like our demonstration get organized, and in the same sequence, how opposition occurs. For most activities, someone floats an idea over salmon tacos at Leon's and by a day or two later, after it circulates person to person though Adolphus, people are either on board or they're not. No one follows up. No one coordinates. Not officially, I mean. People show up or they don't. There's not a ton to do up here, other than the things you do to survive the weather, so most halfway decent ideas get traction without anyone having to step too hard on the gas.

Sometimes things do fall flat. Sometimes someone shows up for something and he or she is the only one there. More often than not when that happens, the person who shows up is the person who floated the idea in the first place, and was so caught up in it that he or she didn't notice no one else was buying in. In a town this small, if you're paying attention, you can pretty much catch the mood to do or not do something right from the get go.

A few mornings before our demonstration, sitting at Leon's when the whole thing got hatched, I was pretty sure there'd be a decent showing. Fighting foreign wars is not high on most Adolphans' list of things they want to just let go by without response. Overall I'd say we're a pretty peace loving bunch, most of us, and basically liberal, but with a streak of fiscal conservatism tossed in, especially when it comes to spending tax dollars on things of no immediate local benefit. It was Mac who reminded us that there were more serious threats to the security of Adolphus than Iraq, and that, "the whole 'dominos of democracy,' enterprise as the Neo-Cons described it, seemed pretty far-fetched." It seemed worse than far-fetched to me.

There were four of us having breakfast with Mac that morning when we reached a consensus about a demonstration: me, Missy Wiggins, the town librarian and my sometimes bridge partner, and Walt Ruhl, a retired bush pilot. Sue-Ellen Allen, the town manager, was also there, but no one expected her to go on the march. She'd be in her office all day as usual, devoted to her duties, slim as her portfolio was. It was her view that as the town's only elected official, she needed to maintain what she called "a presence in the office," in case something came up. Something rarely did.

Allison and Lea were there too, of course, buzzing around, grilling eggs and pancakes and serving coffee. There were a decent number of other people in the café, maybe a half dozen, in singles and pairs. Lea probably spoke for all of us at the table when she joined our conversation between pouring refills and called the President a "disingenuous ass-wipe who just wants to prove to his daddy his balls have dropped." I would not have said ass-wipe.

Adolphus, over the twenty-four years I have lived here, has always been more than tolerant of people with extreme views. There are a few hard-core survivalists here, a few apocalyptics, and some super patriots who fled the lower forty-eight because they think America is going to hell in a hand-basket and that white people like them are being oppressed by fill in the blank: Arabs, Muslims, Jews, blacks, foreigners of other stripes, women, you name it. There are a few vets who fought in Desert Storm or another of our recent wars who tend to be unblinkingly positive about anything the armed forces are sent to do. Though there is little open argument about certain kinds of deep held but hard to debate views, occasionally one of these guys – they are always guys

– shows up at a town meeting or parks himself in Leon's and holds forth, and we all get to hear what he thinks.

Daniel Silk was one of them. He was imposing, muscle-bound, and aggressive, and if he was in a mood to press his point, he was hard to shake off. He served in Desert Storm, and was one of the hell-in-a-hand-basket moralists. He took on Lea and Allison once when I was eating dinner, yelling that "without guys like me defending your rights, chicks like you couldn't do the things you do." He wasn't specific about whether he meant their sexual practices or the fact that they were women entrepreneurs in a pretty macho wilderness town, but after he left that time, Lea wanted to ban him from the café. Allison prevailed on her not to.

"He's a customer, and keeping him out if he wants to come in is going to take more work than shutting him up if he gets out of line once he's here. Everyone knows what he's like. He's not likely to lose us any business. What would the point of banning him be?" That was during tourist season too, when there actually was a risk of losing customers, but one of the reasons I felt the way I did about Allison was her kindness. She was as Christian a lesbian Jew as you were ever likely to find.

When he figured out what we were cooking up over breakfast the morning we planned the march Silk erupted. "You cunts need to stop berating the president. He's a better man than you'll ever be." He included us all, men and women, in the insult. Why he thought he needed to say it in a way that would especially offend Lea and Allison, not to mention Missy and Sue-Ellen, I don't know. Despite his attitude toward them, and whatever feelings they harbored about him, the women remained unfailingly decent to him, as difficult a customer as he sometimes was, and they didn't deserve the anger or the trash talk.

I hated getting into it with him, but he was over the line and I told him so. I had stood up to him a couple of times before, mostly to quiet him down. If he came into the

157

café and started up with someone, it was hard to enjoy a peaceful meal and a good conversation, which is all I ever wanted to have at Leon's. It was just coincidence that he was at Leon's the morning we made the peace march plan, but he acted as if God himself had sent him in to oppose what he called our "anti-Americanism," and he didn't respond particularly well to the idea of our gathering up our fellow citizens for an anti-war demonstration.

"It's a good god damned thing I stopped in here this morning or no one would have called you on your shit." When I stood up to go over and try to get him to pipe down, I saw his dander go up. I walked up to his table and spoke to him in my calmest voice.

"Hey, Daniel. You need to cool it."

"You going to tell people lies about how them A-rabs are just another kind of people? They're butchers. I saw it with my own eyes. I was there. They hate us, and they'd just as soon gut you as look at you."

"We all know how you feel, but you need to stop shouting. That was a private conversation that didn't concern you." That only cranked him up more.

"It sure as hell did concern me. All we have between us and the Taliban are a few thousand troops and those Navy boys flying planes full of smart bombs over the no-fly zone. So I'm calling you out, you and your fucking peace parade." He was standing now, and I dreaded what was about to happen. I took another step toward him, but he put his hand on my chest and stopped me. "What do you think you're gonna do, Grandpa? Throw me out of here? You think you can do that, go ahead and try."

"I came over to ask you in the nicest way possible not to use insulting language about the folks in this café. We'd like to eat our breakfast in peace."

We stood face to face for a long minute with his hand pushing against my shoulder. Then he tossed his napkin on to his plate, shoved me out of his way, and marched out the door. He did not bother to pay. I thought about hollering after him that he had to take care of his check, but decided it was the better part of valor, not to mention better for my personal well-being, if I just picked it up myself. I reached down and plucked it off the table, but Lea came up behind me and grabbed it out of my hand. She knew what I was about to do; I had done it before.

"Not on your life," she said.

Lea and Allison founded Leon's Grill about fifteen years ago. The name was a joke since there was no man named Leon, no man at all in fact. The "Le" was from Lea, and the "on" was from the end of Allison. Sometimes salesmen trying to sell them frozen food or restaurant gear or printed placemats would ask to talk to Leon but, the girls explained, Leon was never in. The salesman would have to talk to them.

I count Lea and Allison among my closest friends. They tell people I was the first customer Leon's ever had, but that's a bit of revisionist history. I was one of the first, but I think they were actually serving some touristy type salmon fishermen before I came in, which was, accurate to their retelling, around lunchtime on the day they opened. I had been watching them get the café ready for business for weeks, and I was glad to see the "Welcome. We're Open." sign hanging on their door. There was only one other place to eat in town if you got sick of your own cooking, the restaurant at the Park Service campgrounds. It was a little out of the way for just stopping in midday, and it was closed from after Thanksgiving to the first of May.

If I wasn't the first, I was the first one who came back. Full disclosure: before I understood that she and Lea were a couple, I was immediately attracted Allison. The woman is beautiful, and even now, fourteen years after I first met her, I sometimes find myself fantasizing what it would have been like if things could have been different between us.

For the first few years they knew me, Lea and Allison made it their mission to find me a suitable mate. I had escaped from an unsuitable one, and hoping to put some physical distance between us, I had come up to Adolphus and bought a garage and machine shop that the owner was glad to be selling. I never intended to stay as long as I have. For some of us, however, the siren song of this place is irresistible. For others, a short visit is all they need to clear their heads and retreat back to where life is easier. Because life here is not easy. The five months a year the waterways are ice bound are especially hard, with little coming in or out to disrupt things or create excitement. Preparing for winter is a full-year job. Keeping warm and dry is no joke. A lot of people heat with wood and you need a lot of stacked cords to stay toasty at night. It takes work.

One of the things you give up when you move to small town Alaska from any decent size American city is the abundance of people you might choose to have as friends, or have a long term love affair with, or partner up for life with. If you're choosey it is easy to be lonely. I've never found anyone to hold a candle to what I imagine Allison would be like as a partner, what I see her being with Lea. It's self-defeating, I know, to have an impossible woman as the standard for all future relationships, but there it is.

Now Lea and Allison tell people who ask that I'm one of those old-fashioned confirmed bachelor types. But at first, they would give the third degree to any tourist or traveler they thought was anywhere near the appropriate age for me, and they would try to persuade those women to stay in town if they thought there was a chance in hell I would be interested. They were successful more often than you'd think, and I had relationships with a few of the women they put their thumbscrews to. But nothing took. There were a couple I had hopes for, but in the end the winter, or the lack of fulfilling work, or the low horizon for accomplishment here drove them away. Or I did. I'm not the easiest guy on the planet, I admit that. I am old fashioned in a lot of ways. I want to be the most important thing in the life of the woman I'm with. But I'm also a caretaker type. I want to take charge. I want to do things for people. I grew up opening doors and carrying groceries and saying yes and no mam. It's a Midwestern thing that did not play all that well in New York, where I ended up after I left home. I think at first, my ex found it charming. Then she started to say I was patronizing. Then she said controlling. Finally she said suffocating. I see what she saw. I just never meant it to show anything but deference and care. Which I have learned is something many women, hell, many people, simply don't want.

I think some people who know me only casually think I'm gay. Some people assume Mac and I are a closeted couple. Some think I'm just some strange sexual monk. So be it. Not that it's anyone's business, really.

Lea and Allison and I spend a good amount of time together, playing scrabble or bridge and talking. Those two women are rabid readers, and they have gotten me into the fiction habit as well, and so I am also friends with Missy, who recommends novels from the library, and who joins me as the fourth on contract bridge nights. We make a pretty slamming bridge team, me and Missy; she's steady and calculating, and almost never bids contracts she can't possibly make.

Once when I was in bed with Missy she told me that she loved me but could never in a million years live with me. I wasn't surprised to hear it. We have sex from time to time, when we both sense we need it, but our deal is we never stay over. If the weather's bad enough that going home would be a danger, we each have a second bedroom. We joke sometimes that we should get married and then not live together so we don't drive each other nuts, just so we'd have someone to be there when the chips were down. I tell her that she has me for that anyway, and I hope I have her, no

161

need to turn it into something it isn't. For a while I wished we could get over ourselves about this, but I was pretty sure we wouldn't. Even with this arrangement, we argue a lot. Missy is very independent. Like me, she came to Alaska getting away from someone. I wouldn't ever want her to have to consider leaving here because of me any more than I would want to feel I had to leave so we wouldn't have to cross paths. The negatives of small town life. The limits of proximity. Better to just be friends.

People in Adolphus do a lot of talking. There's a song that imagines a gadget called a "Speculator" that people turn on when they want to talk about something but don't have any real information about it. Everyone here talks about everyone else. I'm as bad as anyone. When Mac and I get together with Lea and Allison, we gossip like we're two old married couples, or maybe Mac and I are more like maiden aunts. Because Leon's is the town gathering place, Lea and Allison tend to know everything juicy before the rest of us. We all eat up the town gossip like it was ice cream. And if there is nothing local to chew on, there's plenty to snark about in a state this screwed up, in a country this divided. I am sure Missy and I and our strange arrangement give people plenty to crank their Speculators up to ten about.

In addition to being politically progressive, Lea and Allison are very civic-minded. They do things for people; they don't just talk about it. They support our little community, and can be counted on in times of crisis. When we have had extreme freezes they deliver food to our shut-ins. They are the first to sound the alarm when the state government in Juneau is about to do something stupid, like approving drilling leases in places where the potential for environmental damage is high. They lead the fight when taking some endangered animal off the protected list is clearly a boneheaded idea meant to help a chemical company exploit a natural resource and the poor animals are in the way. Lea and Allison are perfect examples of lower forty-eight immigrants who have become rabid Alaskans. And like Missy, even more rabid Adolphans. They love this place as much as anyone could.

Lots of people come to Adolphus for a respite from the stark issues that trouble their lives, and then, revived or disappointed, leave. But if it gets its hooks into you, there's no place like it. There's the natural beauty of the place, for one thing. Mountains frame the bay, soaring up to fourteen thousand feet, and are reflected in the ice blue water. Seals and whales are abundant. Four species of raptors live on our shores including two kinds of eagles. Other exotic birds are plentiful. We get puffins and gulls migrating through, and all sorts of land birds along the shore. Tunneling redpolls, dark-eyed juncos, crossbills, pine siskins, and a few species of hummingbird that have adapted to survive the winters here. There are several species of bear, blacks and browns, and there are longhorn sheep and moose. And the sky is brighter with stars on nights when the weather is clear than anywhere I have ever been. If you love the natural world, it is hard not to love it here.

But it's more than the natural beauty that gets ahold of you. Living here does something to one's soul. It changes the way you see people. If you live in a city, there are so many people, if you abandon a friend or someone pisses you off, it's a loss, but there is always someone else coming down the pike. Here, however much you might despise a person, or loathe his or her views, there's some bond that keeps things from tilting too far out of orbit. You know you're going to see them again. You know you're going to have to deal with them. And it's not like the average small town where there's always the option of lighting out on a moment's notice. Because of the winters, getting out is a project. There are no roads to other towns, or places you can go to for a day just to clear your senses, except for those exquisite places that are even less inhabited than here: snowshoeing up some trail to an overlook point, or finding a place to cross country ski. In the winter, getting on a plane is the only way to be somewhere else. Being stuck, choosing to be stuck, means something. For some people, it's unbearable. For others, for me for instance, it's the whole point of staying here. I feel connected here in ways I am not sure I would anywhere else.

There have been about the same number of people in Adolphus the whole time I have lived here, and that isn't very many, three hundred twenty-two at the last census. A few folks leave and a few more arrive, but for most of us, this is where we have chosen to stay. And we know we need each other. As much as we have our differences and might get on each other's nerves, there is a way in which we all silently acknowledge we are in this together, the 'this' being the sometimes daunting task of living away from abundant and available food to buy, entertainment for distraction, even doctors or hospitals to treat injuries and illness. We live without easy access to the hardware that most civilized places offer their inhabitants to fix broken plumbing and locks and lamps and everything else that breaks in houses. We have no auto parts store for hoses, gaskets, or belts, not to mention batteries and other replacement parts. In decent weather, when there's transport, we order things and wait. Otherwise we make do with an array of 'do-fors' we fabricate or supply to our neighbors when material woes arise. Plenty's been the time I've cut a temporary gasket out of a cardboard twelve-pack container to get someone home on a snowmobile. Because woes do arise in a place like Adolphus, maybe more often than they do in places where life is easier, where weather is less harsh, where materials are less often pushed to their limit. Living here, after a while, you get to know things about yourself that you would never know if you could just call a plumber or an electrician or order out for a pizza whenever you needed or wanted one. You learn how much you can do without, why being in a community really matters, how important it is to be able to ask for help, what relying on your neighbor really means. It's not an option. To survive here, when there is a fire, everyone is a fireman.

The morning we agreed we'd march we assembled at the intersection of Straight and New Streets. I'll avoid repeating my usual snark about the brilliant names of our two major thoroughfares. Some of the early arrivals talked through the route, down Straight to the airport highway, loop through the gate, and then back to town the same way. Not that there's a lot of options. There's only a few streets long enough to make it worth taking fifty-odd people on a march.

The corner of Straight and New is the center of town, to the extent Adolphus has anything anyone would call a center. Town's laid out more like a snake sunning itself along the just-slightly-higher-than-sea-level rise between Glacier Bay on the west and the foothills to the Border Range on the east. On the northwest corner of the intersection there is The Wampum Exchange, our grocery and general store. The store was opened in the late 1970's by a couple of sweet and earnest kids who came up here from Pennsylvania. They'd been taught in elementary school that all Native Americans traded with wampum and thought they were honoring the North Pacific First Nations by choosing that name. Those folks are long gone, and when Rob O'Neill bought the store he shortened its name to "The Exchange," because most people who live here year-round were already calling it that. Rob was standing out front of the store when I came up.

"Why don't you join us? Shut down for a couple of hours. Everyone in town with spending cash will be walking with us. Besides, the walk'll do you good." Rob was the only full time citizen of Adolphus who was actually fat. For most of the rest of us, without ready access to as much junk food as we could want down below the place we lived, it took too much calorie-burning work surviving winter for anyone to really pack it on.

"You're probably right."

"So? Stretch your legs."

"I have stuff to do. I need to phone in an order, or I'm not gonna get it on the flight. Besides, I'm not sure where I stand on this Iraq thing. If Saddam has weapons of mass destruction hidden."

"That's the big question, isn't it? You think we should gear up on a hunch?"

He didn't answer, but I already knew his feelings. Rob was another Desert Storm vet, and it pissed him off that we hadn't eighty-sixed Saddam when we had the chance. If he was less pugnacious about the meaning of his military service than Daniel Silk or the vets who fled to Alaska from the lower forty-eight to get as far away as they could from what they saw as "fundamental weaknesses developing in the American character," as one of them told me one day when we were talking politics, Rob did harbor feelings about the value of a strong military, and those feelings surfaced from time to time. He went all out decorating his store in patriotic bunting on Memorial Day and July 4th, both of which were during tourist season admittedly, but still. He was sending a message. I didn't disrespect him for it.

"Keeping a decent winter inventory is a goddamn pain in the ass," he said. "I get a hundred pounds twice a week in winter off that fucking claustrophobic mail plane. If those scaredy-cat pilots decide to fly. One snowflake and they sleep in, those guys. You know what they say? Good enough for government work. Except I'm paying them and they're commercial pilots and running this store isn't government work, and I still have to pay for their mendacity."

"Wow. Mendacity? They're lying about the weather?"

"You know it. Half the time, they could get here no problem. Hey, you know what you really ought to be protesting? The lack of a dedicated supply plane. We need to get us a cargo jet like they used in The Storm, a Starlifter or one of those C-5 behemoths that can carry half a dozen tanks and land in a blizzard or a sandstorm like they were pulling into a parking space at the Mall of America." Rob was originally from Minneapolis and sometimes it came up how much he missed it. "Then we wouldn't run out of stuff."

"That'd be a decent use of surplus military hardware, I'll grant you. But the town can't afford a plane. And The Exchange isn't big enough for that much inventory."

"We could rent a plane, then." He ignored the warehousing problem. "Twice, three times a winter's all we'd need. Maybe we could get subsidized. We got that satellite phone tower at the airport on a Homeland grant. I read there's still money. We're almost like one of those suffering refugee populations they're always rescuing in Africa or somewhere with those giant planes. Bringing in palettes of food and tents? And we're the first line of defense on this coast. We need a healthy populace. We could all get rickets. How would we defeat the Ruskies if we were all diseased?"

"The Ruskies? Who are you, Dr. Strangelove? And I think you mean scurvy. Scurvy is vitamin C, lack of orange juice. Rickets is vitamin D, lack of sunshine. You think we lack sunshine?"

"Fine. When we're out of, what do you eat for breakfast? Steel cut oats? You'll come around. 'Let's rent that plane,' you'll tell me. 'I'm starving to death.'"

"It scares me that you know what everyone in this town eats for breakfast."

"And lunch. And dinner."

The truth of the matter was, Rob already owned a plane. There was a sort of unspoken agreement among townsfolk not to remind him of this fact. It was a bit of a sore point. Rob bought Ruhl's Cessna in a burst of enthusiasm for the idea of flying in his own supplies, an idea he had not quite acted on yet. Rob did not have a pilot's license. He bought the plane thinking either he would hire someone to fly supplies in for him or, as he told nearly everyone in town at one point or another as they shopped in his store, he would "learn to fly that damn thing and do my own wholesale." He added, more ruefully as time went on, "One of these days," which had turned into months and then some. The problem was, there weren't any certified instructors in town, and the pilots who could teach him, who were around in the summer, were too busy actually flying people into the back country to spend time teaching a neophyte the rules and practicalities of aerial navigation. Not to mention that Rob's store hours during tourist season meant he was tied to his cash register pretty much six days a week nine to six. Added to this fact was the issue of Rob's weight, which reduced by over a hundred pounds or so the amount of actual cargo he could carry if he ever got himself airborne. So the plane sat idle for long stretches, with only an occasional rental to help pay for upkeep and maintenance.

The plane was parked in the big hangar at the airport, probably illegally since Rob wasn't paying rent on the hangar space, covered with canvas to keep the windshield from getting pitted when the wind whipped dust under the hangar doors.

"Just be sure when you learn to fly that puddle jumper of yours you are fully stocked with my vittles." I told him, "I wouldn't want you to go to all of that effort and neglect your best long-term customers."

"I'll keep that in mind," he said. I doubted Rob would ever get his pilot's license. And despite his seeming indifference to it, I knew it must still be a thorn in Ruhl's side that his former plane was sitting out there, unused and mostly uncared for.

Walt Ruhl became a bush pilot after he retired from the Air Force, years before I got here. He hauled mail and sometimes people to outpost communities, but mostly made his living ferrying hunters and fishermen into the backcountry. He was the original owner of the Cessna that Rob now kept at the airport. It was an interesting plane. It was an amphibian – a floatplane with pontoons that was also outfitted with bush wheels for runway landings, when one was available. On Ruhl's plane, the floats could be replaced with skids for snow landings. The skids were high quality custom appliances. Pontoon planes with hydraulic wheels were expensive. I knew the plane pretty well because I had flown in it, and because my shop did some welding on the attachments for the snow skids a few seasons back. Ruhl thought the skids would keep him in business year-round. The Cessna had been his pride and joy. "A tri-phibian," he told me once, showing off the lifts that allowed the wheels to jut out from the pontoons. He is affable as they come, Ruhl is, another guy I counted as a friend.

The reason his former plane was sitting unused in the hangar was that he had his license pulled by the FAA two years ago for flying under the influence. He was ratted out by some dentist from Bloomington, Minnesota, who didn't take kindly to the too-close-for-comfort low passes over tall mountains and death-defying landings on isolated lakes, despite having assured Ruhl that he understood the dangers of flying into the backcountry. Ruhl had apparently taken an immediate dislike to this particular punter, probably because he was a condescending asshole, who bragged about his shooting skills and his pay-for-kill African trophies that underhanded guides engineered for him, so Ruhl drank just enough to take the edge off the guy's blabbering, and to get himself a little reckless. The dentist was probably never in danger; Ruhl was a cracker-jack pilot, and frankly half the guys I've flown with up here have taken a slug before they took off just to take the chill off, but this guy had enough clout that he got some congressman to call some bureaucrat who sent some inspectors from Anchorage and it became a big stink on the wire services about the bush pilots taking risks with tourists lives. The national media picked it up and the governor got on his high horse about it, and it ended with them pulling Ruhl's ticket.

The funny thing was, he wasn't bitter about it. He didn't turn into the angry drunk I'm pretty sure I'd have become if someone painted me the way he was painted in the press and then killed my livelihood. He sold his plane to Rob, took his social security and service pension, and walked away. Walt was a solid citizen. He had even been substitute town manager when Sue-Ellen had her gall bladder out a few years ago. No one in town had a bad word to say about him. Except maybe Rob who was pissed that Ruhl wouldn't teach him how to fly his former plane.

"No can do, buddy," I heard Ruhl tell Rob in Leon's one night. "I'm in enough hot water with the Federales. You want me to be teaching you from jail?"

I was pretty sure that even if Walt did teach Rob the rudiments of aerial navigation there would be no jail time to serve. But I knew the real reason he said no. Walt decided that acting like an asshole with that hunter was a sign he needed to change his ways. He was never enough in love with flying to feel not doing it was such a tragedy, so he stopped drinking and packed it in.

Rob shook me off and went back inside the store. I headed down the block past Leon's. The door to the café was open and there was a coffee urn on the front table and some take-out cups that Allison and Lea had set up for anyone who wanted a warm-up before the march. I saw them with Sue and Ruhl standing outside of the building the post office and town manager shared a few yards up Straight. There's a bike rack in front of the Post Office and a snow mobile parking area just beyond it, but in the winter people park wherever they feel like. Not that we have anyone who would enforce parking laws. Or any other laws, for that matter. There are two signed spaces for "official vehicles" alongside of the town manager's office, but no one remembers the town ever having owned any vehicles, official or otherwise. Drunk and disorderly is probably the biggest crime we see, and it's as likely as not it's someone we all know who has gone a little stir crazy in the dead of winter. I think I once heard of someone sleeping off a corker in the post office. But who would have confined him there is beyond me. Mostly people stay home to get wasted. Someone gets that jacked up in public someone else just walks him or her home, and tucks him or her in at his own place.

There hasn't been a violent crime here in all the time I've been here unless you count fistfights as crime, and I've never heard of anything being stolen that wasn't simply borrowed and returned the next day or two. Not that some of our most virulent survivalists don't exude the potential for violence and scare the shit out of people the way Daniel Silk sometimes scared the shit out of me.

We function pretty much without a government, without cops, without most of the artifacts of civic organization, and we do just fine. The town manager deals with all the legal issues of being a municipality. Wikipedia designates Adolphus as "a second class city" but even saying city dignifies things an awful lot. Village is more like what we are, and the town manager is an elected position that might as well be appointed since Sue-Ellen has been doing it uncontested for a long time now. She's good at the job, unstintingly fair-minded, and she gets by on its insanely meager pay. No one has the desire to stand against her in an election. She deals with property and school taxes, which are notoriously low here, and the few obligations this particular municipality has to its citizens. The town gets state oil and gas subsidies, and as an entity we don't really own much.

There's an industrial scale diesel plow for clearing the runways out at the airport that was left here by the Air Force when they stopped using the airport during the Reagan-era base closings. Not that there's usually all that much snow at the airport, either. The town probably owns that by adverse possession now, which as I understand it is the legal version of finders-keepers, but no one seems sure. Every once in a while it breaks down and Sue-Ellen calls someone and a guy flies in from Seattle to do repairs. He bills Alaska Air, and they apparently pay. No one is sure what their relation to the plow is either, though no one wants to poke around under that particular umbrella.

The airport gets busy in the summer. We get two commercial jets a day through here in season, roughly May through September, on a round trip loop from Juneau, when there are enough tourists coming to the Park Service campsite or to the B&Bs in town to make flying a big plane worthwhile. Even though it's scheduled, Alaska Air cancels flights if they're under-booked. We get some charters through in the summer too, and a few private planes with hunters or fisherman. In the winter, if the weather is decent, we get the commuter turbo-prop from Juneau twice a week, the mail plane that Rob hates, that also brings the occasional off-season traveler, usually a Park Service employee or the relative of someone living here, the occasional winter tourist (a species I find particularly curious) and, of course, the supplies and food Rob orders. Nothing big gets delivered in the winter. Big stuff comes in airfreight in season, or by boat or barge before the bay ices up in October.

There's nothing else other than the diesel plow and now Rob's plane in the hangar, which might also be deemed to be the town's by now too, for all anyone knows. It's big enough for a 727 and is also left over from when the Air Force was here. No one has ever seen a jet use it though. When the jets land, they don't even turn off their engines. People exit or board the plane, and dash to and from the terminal, which is a Quonset hut that serves as the gateway to the parking lot. The planes taxi off and get airborne back to Juneau as fast as they can. We have no runway lights, so flying is a daytime, clear weather activity. There's no fuel cache here either, and no repair shop, and way too much

172

sudden weather and tricky wind to spend any extra time on the tarmac. I suppose if really bad weather came up suddenly a jet might get towed into the hangar, if we had a tug to do that, which we don't.

In front of the post office there is a park bench, with a dedication plaque that says, "Russian Wilderness Campground," which is about a thousand miles to the south, on the border between California and Oregon. No one in town has a clue how that got here.

By about ten fifteen, enough of us had gathered for the demonstration that there was a consensus we ought to start out. If there were stragglers they'd catch up.

"We're going to head out Straight, walk to the airport, and then walk back," Allison told the crowd, standing on the Russian Wilderness bench, though the announcement was pro forma. It wasn't like our route was a surprise or had been a secret up to that moment. "There's coffee and go cups in the café, and fresh fried donuts if the early birds haven't eaten them all already. Otherwise, let's say we set off in five minutes or so." I was disappointed that the donuts had all been snarfed-up before I got there. "Really good," was what Mac told me. "I had two."

"You're a greedy bastard," I told him. He brushed the powdered sugar off of his mustache using the back of his hand in an exaggerated gesture. I loved Mac. He was a great guy, the kind of friend you could trust with your tools and your wife, if you have a wife, which neither of us did. He was my neighbor and my hiking and kayaking buddy, and probably knew me as well as anyone in Adolphus other than Missy, or Allison and Lea, but only because I hung out in their café more than in Mac's kitchen. Still, if cups of coffee and slugs of whiskey consumed in each location were vying against each other, the competition would have been awfully close.

Mac came up to Alaska in the early 90's after he "retired." He was forty-eight when he arrived. He'd been an investment banker who made a killing on some startup and at a certain point he'd just gotten sick of the money managing game and cashed out. His wife at the time, a New York socialite, thought he had lost his marbles and divorced him. Their settlement made him poorer, but not poor, and he spent his time perfecting his hobby as a wildlife photographer, eventually getting good enough to publish in *National Geographic* and *Nature* and to get assignments to photograph endangered animals and their habitats all over the world. He shot the prize-winning photos of the mother polar bear and her cubs that became the symbol of rising oceans and global warming; you see them everywhere now, all over the Internet and even on tee shirts. He also took almost all of the published shots of that orca that was transported from captivity in the Mexican amusement park to his reintroduction to the sea off the Oregon coast. Those pictures helped raise millions for animal rescue. He had a gift for getting images of animal behavior that had human resonance without making the animals cutesy caricatures. He managed to make the consequence of human action on our fellow creatures deeply and visibly moving.

In terms of our impact on the war and even on the hearts and minds of people in our town, there wasn't much likelihood we were going to recruit an army of additional anti-war protestors from along our line of march, despite Daniel Silk's concern, or realistically have much influence on anyone. The point was more to have covered enough distance to feel we had done something, made a small statement with our effort, and made our feelings known, though I suppose in most ways this could have occurred if we had simply all given a show of hands about our objection to Bush's intentions while standing at the corner of Straight and New or sitting in the school lunchroom where we had town meetings. But marching was a way of having the semblance of an active political life in a place where most national politics feel decidedly remote. Except that our tax dollars would be supporting whatever happened, and our kids were likely as any to get sent off into the sinkhole some lefty pundits were predicting Iraq would become. We had a few kids who were in high school ROTC and a few more neighbors who were in the reserves. If they called up a reserve troop or a National Guard battalion we would be represented in the same proportion as everyone else in the country, and if the numbers were small, the impact on the town was potentially large. Three or four skilled people pulled out of a town of under four hundred for a year or more is big. No one gathered to march wanted any of our citizens to have to go.

It would take the better part of an hour to make the circle all the way up to the airport and back. We had all driven or hiked this route before, lots of times, and most of us had marched it, protesting one thing or another. There had been a march against opening protected wilderness to oil drilling as recently as last December, though only a handful of people turned out for that one. Oil drilling is more controversial here than foreign war, though it shouldn't be in my view. But people up here get benefits from our oil riches, and it's hard to talk some folks out of them. Doesn't matter to those people that things like the Valdez happen, or there are pipeline spills. Doesn't matter that fossil fuels are killing our planet.

An hour walk in a town the size of ours, in wind as wet and biting as it was, seemed like a reasonable duration. Something you could take your kids on and not feel like it hadn't been enough. I don't have kids, of course, but a fair number of the folks who turned out do. There were eight kids, with ten total parents, some singles and some couples. I wonder sometimes what it was like for kids who grew up here, what it would have been like for me to have grown up here. I came from the Midwest, from Colby, Kansas, a town so landlocked I used to dream of oceans, a place I was jet propelled to get out of. I blasted out of there at eighteen, and didn't turn my afterburners off for fifteen years. But if you had asked me during any of those years if I thought I would end up spending the following twenty-five in a small town in Alaska I'd have laughed in your face.

The kids I've watched grow up here are pretty independent. They're outdoors kids, self-entertaining kids. That part is not a lot different from what it was for me as a kid. My dad had a mobile machine shop and went from farm to farm repairing harvesters and plows, welding broken axles and straightening bent rods of various kinds. I knew a lot of farm kids, but I wasn't like them. I liked to read, mostly popular science and other magazines that inspired dreaming. Not a lot of the kids here are readers, according to Missy, who knows from running the library. People have TV's and DVD players. But I suspect that our kids are less likely to be couch potatoes than kids in cities. Most of them do chores, like I did as a kid. When I got old enough I started working with my dad. That's how I know what I know, and how I have kept myself alive up here. Mine is the only machine shop and garage in town. I sell gas, to the few cars in the summer and the snowmobilers in the winter. I weld and repair things, from sled blades to winches on trawlers. I keep a good stock of hoses and clamps, belts and gaskets, and I have decent basic fabricating tools. I'll never get rich from what I do, but I like it, and I'm good at it, and it keeps me in parkas and pants.

I'm not sure if most kids work with their parents anywhere else, but here there's enough to do keeping one's house or car or plow or snowmobile in repair that having an extra set of hands usually helps. A lot of kids here grow up handy. I have no problem finding reasonably skilled helpers if I need an assistant on a particularly tricky job.

The difference between growing up here and growing up on the flat Kansas interior is the beauty quotient. Kids here don't look out the window and wonder if the whole world is as dull as what they see stretching out from their front yard. At its best, Colby, Kansas, had a golden hue when the wheat was high. At its worst it was dry and dusty, flat and featureless. The people became the same way. My parents were born and died in Colby. A big deal for them was a trip to Hays, Salina, Topeka, or Kansas City. All of which, in most ways, were the same place. Here, you turn around and the world is different. Water, mountains, blue glaciers, fields of wildflowers. Do towering mountains inspire towering dreams? I want to believe they do. The opposite of how I felt when I was growing up, that everything as tall as a corn stalk would end up being cut down and brought to earth. But maybe it's the other way; endless expanse of nothing made my imagination bold.

As we walked, there weren't many people on the road to see our signs and banners. There are never many people on the road, so we weren't expecting throngs like those who pour out of buildings to watch mid-day protests street-side in major cities in the lower forty-eight. There, the curious come out to see the parade, and people watching cheer or jeer the politics of the marchers. Here, there were no buildings lining our route, no lunchtime office workers looking for diversion while they munch their sandwiches. Still, despite the lack of population, there's a strange thing about this place. Whenever anything does go on in Adolphus in public, people do come out to watch. Half the time stuff that is supposed to be happening in complete privacy draws attention, like when Jojo Allen took Rob for some romance behind the old cannery last year. Place's been closed for two years, not a soul lives on that road, and still someone in town saw them go up the road together, and must have seen what they were doing, because it was known all over town almost before they were back. It was embarrassing for Jojo, who wasn't even married to Burt Hull anymore, though some people acted like she was, mostly the people who thought Burt was too good for her. I couldn't have cared less. I thought Jojo and Rob would make a good couple, which turned out to be true since they're still seeing each other. My point is, on the peace march, we expected to have only a few people watching, but that didn't mean we didn't expect to have an impact. Mac always took pictures of Adolphus events, and sent them to the newspapers in Anchorage, Fairbanks, and Juneau, and they were usually published. That was one of the reasons we were all in the paper. Mac's shots were always interesting, as good as any news journalism shots, even though he hated the idea of being thought of as a photojournalist. The heart attack gave his photos of the march a personal interest hook, and all three newspapers published them with stories about the protest and his collapse. Then somehow the wire services picked up the story, and all of the sudden we were in *The New York Times*: me, Lea, Allison, Missy, and, of course, Walt Ruhl, who was wearing his old Air Force jacket as a sort of "warriors for peace" statement, and about an eighth of the rest of the residents of Adolphus.

I think that was also part of what caught the attention of the *Times*. Demographically, we had a very high proportion of protestors. Fifty-one out of three hundred twenty-two permanent residents. "Get a load of those numbers, Mr. President," was how I personally interpreted it. I read somewhere that every person who turns out for a protest march represents four who agree with the principles being expressed but don't show up for various reasons. If that's true then two hundred and four people out of three hundred twenty-two residents didn't think we had either the right or a good reason to go into Iraq. And of course, with hindsight, all of us were right. It was just a debacle, a waste of treasure and lives as they now say, and it was all based on lies our leaders knew were lies. But we didn't know that then. Our opposition was philosophical. We simply didn't think our country should be undertaking that war.

In many ways, Mac's photos of the march that day were a pretty complete portrait of the town. At first, I was annoyed at him for not walking with me. We had plenty to talk about. We were planning a trip south to the Bay Area, partly to get out of the cold and rain for a couple of weeks and partly to attend a big ecology-themed photography show at the de Young, in which Mac was going to have some work. He wanted to go incognito, just to see it, and I wanted to stand him to a few drinks to celebrate his success and tell him what a good friend he had been to me, not that he didn't already know that. Our travel plans were incomplete, but every time we talked about it, he was vague.

"What the hell is wrong with you?" I asked him the weekend before the march, when we were looking up hotels on the Internet. "To get a picture of the bristlebird doing its mating dance in Borneo you'll sleep standing up for four nights, but you can't decide between a Hyatt and a Hilton in one of the most commodious cities in the world? You see I do pay attention to where you tell me you have gone to take pictures."

"Bristlehead."

"What?"

"In Borneo. Bristlehead not bristlebird."

"Whatever."

He shrugged. "I was thinking maybe we'd go all out, spend a little dough, treat ourselves to something special. I'm tired of chain hotels. That's where they book me when I'm on assignment. I'll tell you, the one thing I miss from my banker days is how I traveled. First class. Eighteen-hundred thread count sheets, personal valets, silver coffee service, plush robes, all your needs anticipated."

"I have a limited income. You check into the Fairmount. I'll stay down the street in the Holiday Inn and be just as happy with polyester sheets, scratchy towels, and the breakfast bar in the lobby – as long as someone other than me is cooking, pouring the coffee, and making the bed. You give me those little individually wrapped soaps and throwaway shampoo bottles and I'm in hog heaven. I don't need a personal valet or satin pillow shams. Or you can order me a croissant and some fresh-squeezed orange juice for breakfast and I'll meet you in your room."

"If we go to see my show this deal's on me. You're not too proud to let me pay for your hotel room, are you Mr. Limited Income?"

"Can you come up with something that's maybe half way in the middle? A decent boutique place? Someplace quaint?"

"That's bullshit. Those places are cubbyholes tricked up to make the stingy feel special. That's Democrat luxury. You think a small, well-decorated room means you are being all ecological, not flaunting your privilege. Except in this case, I'm bucking for real Republican overkill opulence. And besides, I want to get laid. You think I want to bring some classy woman back to a walk-in closet with glassed-in bathroom and try to convince her it's sexy that I can see her taking a piss from my bed? I want her to see the size of my checkbook in the room I'm checked into."

"I'll skip the fill-in-the-blank size compensation joke. You can get laid just as successfully at a Wyndham or a Holiday Inn."

"Not by the kind of woman I'm planning to go after."

"Didn't you tell me you were done with socialites?"

"Fine. You pick up a French fry gobbler and I'll pick up a *fois gras* nibbler. We'll see who has better sex and a better story in the morning. You know there was a study, right? Republicans have more orgasms."

"I read that study. They also have a lot less sex. You have to factor that in to your pick-up plans."

Of course, this was all trash talk. If either of us were able to pick up anyone, it would probably be sheer dumb luck. We were two slightly-gone-to-seed guys with more hope than sex appeal, and we both knew it. We were average late-middle-aged men, going soft and gray, and if we were full of bravado to each other, we were, I believe, at least honest with ourselves, leaky prostates, bad knees and all. The male bullshitting we engaged in was juvenile. Mac had the benefit of being successful and well-known as an artist, but whatever his fantasy, he certainly wasn't going to talk anyone into bed because he took beautiful pictures of wrecked eagle nests. Still we fell into this banter easily, after a lifetime of practicing guy talk. We never said this stuff in public, not that every woman on the planet doesn't know that men say these things, and not that women don't have their own version of the same banter. None-the-less, we'd both have been mortified if Allison or Lea or Sue-Ellen or Missy heard us talk this way.

But that still left the real details of the trip to be decided. I thought we could solve some of the logistics while walking, and I had a few places I researched that I thought might satisfy both of us written down for Mac to take a look at. We had had some other tentative conversations, one about renting a car and driving the coast highway from San Francisco to L.A., and spending a few days there. His photo agency had an office in L.A., and he liked to drop in on them every once in a while "to remind them that there's an actual person behind the lens at the address they send checks to," he said, and so that was on the possible itinerary. I wanted to go to the Getty and the Los Angeles County Museum, but we were also talking about being in L.A. during Academy Awards week when hotel rooms were going to be at a premium, especially the kind of hotel rooms he was talking about.

When he started to run ahead of the march like we were the subjects of a photo study, I got annoyed. Once we were beyond the cluster of buildings that made up the town proper, he was out walking ahead of the line, or parallel to it on the other side of the street. He was, it turned out, trying to get a shot that included the whole line of march, lit from the front (we were walking in a generally easterly direction).

After the pictures were published, everyone in town had interpretations about the position of people on the march, what it meant that X had walked with Y, or who was next to whom, or who was obviously avoiding whom, or who was where in the line of march.

When Mac collapsed, at first no one realized he was struggling. We were at about the halfway point between town and the airport. Allison and Lea were leading the parade, and Walt Ruhl was at the tail when a ten-year-old Chevy F-150 came roaring up from the direction of town. The truck's got its suspension jacked way up and big, noisy exhaust pipes curved up over the bed. We all knew whose truck it was; it was Daniel Silk's. All of the vehicles in Adolphus were ferried in at one time or another, and residents get so they know everyone by his or her car. Someone once said it was a little like Havana here the way old cars are kept running. I guess I'm more than partially responsible for that. Someone here gets a new car, everyone notices. But the flip-side is that there isn't really too far to go to get anywhere, so cars last forever if they're decently maintained. No one in a car is ever just passing through.

Silk was speeding. The state limit is fifty-five, and he was way more than ten miles over that when he passed Lea and Allison. He drove ahead maybe another hundred yards, and then we all saw his brake lights go on. My first thought was that his interest was the women at the head of the line, and I was prepared to jog up there if he started any funny business or gave them any guff, not that they couldn't handle pretty much anything anyone dished out, but that was my reflex. But then he is racing backwards, driving in reverse past them, past me in the middle of the march, all the way to the end of line, where he stopped next to Walt Ruhl.

"You're a disgrace, you know it?" he shouted out his window. "You fucking drunk." Ruhl ignored him, and kept walking, but the guy would not let up. "You were military. Why are you walking with these faggots? You're a disgrace to your uniform. Take off that jacket, at least. No one should see you in that."

I didn't hear any of this, of course. It's all from what Missy told us afterward, when she reported the conversation to me, Lea, Allison, and Sue-Ellen, who were waiting in the cafe for a phone call from the hospital in Juneau. Missy had been walking with Ruhl. At first she thought Daniel was pissed enough that he might actually try to take the jacket off of Ruhl's back. "He was fuming," she told us.

The conversation through the car window to Ruhl at the back of the line of march pretty much stopped things cold. We were all aware that something was going on, and people bunched up on the road and turned back to see what it was. That was when Ruhl saw that Mac was struggling.

Ruhl handed off his "No Invasion of Iraq" sign to one of the other marchers, and started to run toward Mac. Missy told us, "At first people thought he was running away from Silk, or that he was coming to get into it with him, but he ran around the front of Daniel's truck and sprinted down the road."

Silk, apparently also thinking that Ruhl was coming for him, had slammed his truck into park and opened the door. I saw him get out, but then stop his forward progress when Ruhl ran by him, at which point I turned myself to look at what Walt was running toward, and took off as well.

Mac's collapse was a slow motion corkscrew. He tried to protect his camera as he fell, bringing it into his chest, instinctively toward the pain. He teetered for a moment, and then he went down, smashing the lens on the macadam as he did.

For a minute afterward, there was chaos. Silk got back into his truck, and started to pull forward. The marchers, who were now bunched up in the middle of the street, broke apart and scattered. No one was sure what was going to happen, but I think some of us feared things were going to get ugly.

When he was alongside of Mac, Silk threw open his door and shouted at the people around Mac. "Let me through." Then he was on his knees next to him. He pulled Mac's broken camera over his head and handed it off to someone. Then he pulled a knife off of his belt. There was a moment when there were too many conflicting images to process or understand. I am sure I was not the only one who assumed Silk was about to stab Mac. But then he leaned close to Mac's ear and asked him something, then deftly sliced Mac's shirt open and started doing chest compressions. "He's having a heart attack. I've seen this before. We need to keep him alive until we can fly him to Juneau."

I was probably not the only one who knew at that moment that we were in serious trouble. The only plane on the ground at the Adolphus airport was the one Ruhl had flown for years, which was now owned by Rob. I had no idea if the plane was currently air-worthy, when it had last been used, if it had been serviced recently, or if it even had enough fuel in it to get to Juneau. Nor did any of us know what configuration the plane was in. It was likely to have been on its pontoons with the wheels poking through, since as far as I knew no one had rented it for winter flying. I was pretty sure Rob would have mentioned if someone had. But I knew I could be mistaken, that the skids could be on, and if they were it would take time to get them off for a runway rather than snowfield takeoff.

And even if it was flight-ready, it was certainly cold, and would need to be warmed up for a while before anyone pushed its engines through a takeoff. And who would fly it? Ruhl was the only pilot around, and it was illegal for him to get behind the controls.

From out of the crowd things began to appear. Allison came up and pulled off her down jacket, rolled it and placed it under Mac's head. Lea began to usher the kids who had been on the march away from the scene of Mac being given CPR. Someone rolled another jacket under Mac's feet.

184

Allison was leaning down by Mac's head whispering to him, telling him to be strong, to hang in there, that help was on the way, that everything was going to be all right, saying anything she thought would comfort him.

Daniel Silk continued to keep up his compressions on Mac's chest, counting out loud. "One-two-three-four-five-six. Two-two-three-four-five-six." After he got through the four-two-three-fours he said, "Listen, someone needs to count for me. I need to do ten sets of these a minute. So you look at your watch and say the numbers out loud so I can hear. Meanwhile, I am going to give you instructions. When you get to ten, start over at one."

Ruhl jumped on the counting immediately. This was something they had each learned in the service, putting aside everything else for combat emergencies.

Silk said, "The keys to my truck are in my left-hand jacket pocket. Someone who knows how to drive a stick needs to take Ruhl to the airport."

I chimed in. "He can't fly. He has no license."

"Fuck that. He's what we got. You want to save this man? Someone's gotta take him to Juneau."

I said, "Someone needs to tell Rob, get his keys, find out what kind of shape that plane is in. I don't want to lose both of them taking off in that thing if it hasn't got enough juice to get across the bay." There was panic in my voice, and I knew everyone heard it.

Ruhl said, "I have keys, seven-two-three-four-five-six." Everyone looked at him. "I kept a set. Eight-two-three-four-five-six. For old times' sake, nine-two-three-four-five-six. "Ten-two-three-four-five-six. When I turned over the plane to Rob. I kept a set." He started over at one. The counting continued with Silk compressing Mac's chest as the plans unfolded.

"All right. Go to the airport and call Rob from there," Silk said. "Who's gonna drive? Someone who knows how to handle a stick. I don't want my gears torn up."

185

At nearly the same moment, Missy Wiggins and I both said, "I can drive a stick." She said, "My first job was driving lumber haulers for Boise Cascade."

"That settles it. Missy Drives. I want you here," Silk told me, "to spell me on the compressions. She's too small for it. Ruhl is shotgun to the airport. When you get there, call Rob and get his permission if you think it's worth taking the time. Okay. Next. Lea. There are two defibrillators in town. I have one in my place; there's one at the town office. There's also one at the airport. When you find Rob, tell him to find someone with a car to bring the one from the office back here. Let's hope the damn things are charged. There's an indictor on the case. If it isn't, have him go up to my place. It's not locked. Be careful of my dog. And Missy, bring the one back from the airport. We'll try to light him up here on battery. If that doesn't work we can plug it back in when we get back to the hangar. Ruhl, you can deal with the FAA after you fly this man across. What do you think is the worst they're gonna do to you? Ground you?"

"Someone else count," Ruhl said, breaking off.

I picked up where Ruhl stopped. "Six-two-three-four-five-six." I was impressed with how organized Silk was, how able to take charge he was, and how decent his plans seemed. Given his rants and his drinking, I would not have guessed he had it in him.

"Missy, once you drop Ruhl at the airport, and you pick up the defibrillator in the terminal, get back here ASAP. Ruhl'll warm up the plane, we'll get this man stable, and load him into the truck and get him over there. And I'll fly with you and him to Juneau. Also, Lea, while you're in town, find some aspirin. It'll help him. Rob has it in the store."

Mac was drained of color, but he was awake. He was letting whatever was being done to him go on with little protest. I figured he was in enough pain that whatever fight he had, he was using it to maintain himself in the realm of the living. At least I hoped that was what he was doing.

186

Silk kept up his compressions. I counted. Allison kept talking to Mac. "You're gonna be fine. There's a plan. Just keep it together. I know you're in pain. We're doing everything we can. It's gonna be fine. Don't check out on us now." It was patter, but Mac seemed fixated on it. He looked into Allison's eyes and avoided mine. I was just as glad that he did. I wasn't sure I wouldn't have burst into tears.

After Lea got the kids away from the place where Mac had fallen, and gotten them and their parents started on the walk back to town, the peace march now obviously over, she set off at a dead run back toward town where we had started.

I don't know when in the sequence I noticed that the temperature had dropped and it had started to snow, but all of the sudden it was coming down pretty hard. It was cold enough that it was going to stick on the road, and I worried about Missy's skills as a driver. It was just free form worrying. She'd been driving in snow for years. Then I worried that the snow would make taking off more dangerous, flying completely treacherous, landing in Juneau a hazard. I knew that crosswinds over the Lynn became even trickier in bad weather, and the snow blowing high off the Chilkats could disorient a pilot so completely he could fly straight into them while thinking he was a mile above. I knew that Ruhl knew how to fly in bad weather, or that he used to, but that did not comfort me. I worried that pilots got rusty if they didn't fly for a while, in that use-it-or-lose-it way.

I heard the roar of Silk's truck engine start and looked up to see Missy peeking up from behind the steering wheel. Compared to Silk, she was tiny, and even with the seat adjusted all the way forward, from ground level she looked like a little kid playing in her daddy's car. But soon she and Ruhl were speeding off toward the airport.

187

Once everyone was deployed – and deployment was what it was – there was only counting and waiting. Silk kept doing compressions, and Allison kept sweet-talking Mac about staying alive.

"You fucked up the protest, Mac," she whispered to him. "How are we going to stop this country from going to war if you can't complete a simple protest walk?" He managed a grim smile at her. I wondered if she was saying that to piss Daniel off, but he ignored her and continued to press rhythmically down on Mac's chest. He was in a kind of zone, I think, where there was nothing but this duty to perform. We were no longer political adversaries. We were simply neighbors relying on each other. It occurred to me that we would have done the same for him if he had fallen into need, despite anything we felt about him.

"When you are done with this scary shit you're pulling here, we are going to make you walk this road again, Mister," Allison cooed to him. "You're not getting away with copping out on your political duty. And we're going to make you carry the heavy end of a banner, too."

In town, Lea could not find Rob. Apparently I had guessed right that everyone with money was on our little protest hike and no one was shopping, so Rob had closed up and gone somewhere. His store was locked up tight and the lights were off. There was a handwritten "Back Soon" sign on the shade, but Lea wasn't sure the sign wasn't always there, just not something she paid attention to when the store was obviously open. She checked around the back of the building where there was a buzzer for his apartment above the store, but there was no answer. She ran up the outside stairs and banged on his door, but he clearly wasn't home. She knew it wasn't worth spending any more time looking for him. He was probably at JoJo's, but she decided that running out to her place and then rousting Rob out and getting him to come back to the store, all to ask him if Ruhl could use the plane, was a waste of time. For some reason, he and JoJo still pretended they weren't seeing each other when everyone knew they were. Lea gave up the idea of getting his keys, or getting permission to fly his plane, and headed over to the town office to get the defibrillator. She needed to find someone with a car to take her back to where Mac was lying in the road.

When she passed the café, she saw Sue-Ellen coming out of the town office. Sue-Ellen had a car. "There's been an accident," Lea told her. "Mac's had a heart attack, or some sort of attack, and we need to take a defibrillator out to him and then fly him to Juneau."

"Who's with him?"

"Daniel Silk is doing CPR." Other people from the march were starting to drift back into town now, and Sue-Ellen understood how things had gone. "You have aspirin in your office?"

In the car, on the way back out to where Silk was working on Mac, Lea told Sue-Ellen the rest of the plan. She also asked her, "Don't you have some municipal authority so that we can get a plane flown in from Juneau if Ruhl can't use Rob's plane? Can't you declare a state of emergency? And can you pardon Ruhl if the Feds get up his ass?"

Sue-Ellen was practical as always. "Let's save Mac first, and worry about the consequences and niceties afterwards."

Lea told me later that she told Sue-Ellen, "This is when I start to doubt the sanity of my whole life and every choice I've ever made."

Sue-Ellen didn't bite. "Don't. We all know what it means living here, especially Mac." She told Lea to shut up. She needed to concentrate on the road, which was icing up fast.

The rest of the ride, Lea told me, they were silent. There was too much to worry about to get too far ahead of themselves, and both women knew it.

At the airport, Missy drove around the circle at the entrance and realized that she couldn't drive out to the hangar because there was a chain link fence around the runway.

"I never think about this fence," she told Ruhl.

"There's a service gate around the grid," he told her, and she swung around and sped off toward it. When they got there Missy pulled up next to it. "I can squeeze through," Ruhl told her. "I used to do it all the time. I'll get the defibrillator then I'll get this baby cranked up."

"How will we get Mac through the gate?"

"There's a key inside the hangar. It'll be open when you get back."

It took less than seven minutes for Sue-Ellen to drive to where Daniel was working on Mac, and less than ten for Missy to drive the defibrillator back from the other direction. On the street, Allison and I had made a kind of tent out of my jacket so that the snow was not falling on Mac's face. Allison still leaned close to his ear, now singing to him. She was in the middle of *What a Wonderful World*, having already sung *Bye Bye Blackbird* and *My Funny Valentine*. For a moment, lost in her voice, I had a pang of jealousy that she was singing to Mac. "I see trees of green, red roses, too, I see them bloom, for me and for you. And I think to myself, what a wonderful world." It was another moment when I regretted that she and I would never be a couple. It occurred to me in that moment that hers was the voice I would want to hear singing in my ear if I was dying.

I think we all saw the moment Mac slipped from consciousness to something below it. His eyes had been closed for a while, but his breathing had been regular and then it wasn't. Silk caught my eye, and shook his head. I thought he was going to stop, but he went on, and I went on counting.

Missy and Sue-Ellen pulled up at nearly the same moment, and all of the sudden Silk was barking orders again. "Get that thing set up and charging. We might only have one

190

or two shots at this." Sue-Ellen, who was new on the scene and warmer than the rest of us, was on the ground with the box.

"What's the status of the plane?" Silk asked Missy.

"When I drove off, Walt was headed toward the hangar. I didn't wait to see if he got the engine started or if there was gas in it or anything. But I'm worried. No one is clearing the runway and there's already a fair amount of snow on it. I'm not sure he can get airborne, and I'm not sure once he does he can fly in this."

"He's gonna have to," Daniel said. "Is that charged?"

"Says it is." Sue-Ellen hovered over it, keeping the snow off.

"All right. Let's do this." Silk took the leads and laid them on Mac's chest. The machine did some analysis. "Okay. Stand back," he told everyone. "Everyone clear? Do it."

Sue-Ellen hit the button. There was a pop, and the shock made Mac's body jump. He seemed to ripple like a wave had travelled through him. But when he flattened out he did not seem to be doing any better. In a moment, when the machine beeped, it became clear that the shock had not restored his heart rhythm. We were all clenched tighter than a fist. "Again," Silk said.

The second shock had the desired effect. The machine indicated that his heart was beating somewhere near properly, though we all knew he could fail again. "Let's get him into the truck. On three. One. Two." On three, Mac floated up on six pairs of hands: mine, Sue-Ellen's, Allison's, Lea's, Missy's and Daniel Silk's. We carried him to the truck, and slid him onto the back seat. Daniel squeezed in next to him, and Missy got back behind the wheel.

Missy said, "Thank God for king cabs." Then there was the sound of doors being slammed and they were off. Lea, Allison, Sue-Ellen and I stood on the road watching the truck's tail lights fade as it sped toward the airport. All four of us were crying.

"Oh God," Allison said. "I can't stand this."

Sometimes if the snows come early but snow skids aren't on, floatplanes are landed on the grass next to the runway and towed onto trailers and winterized that way. Ruhl was relieved to find the plane in the hangar and on its wheels. He didn't do a walk-around, but got right into the cockpit. There was no time to pre-heat the engine. He went by instinct through his pre-flight routine. Switches on, flaps and elevators set, rudder trimmed for takeoff, then ignition on. He revved his former plane up to its full RPM's. The engine needed to warm up some before he took off in this weather. He knew it was going to be fighting the cold all the way to Juneau. He had no idea what kind of shape the pilots who had rented it had left it in, and he was pretty sure it hadn't had a full service check-out since he had put the keys into Rob's hands. He told me later that "things sounded okay, but things could change fast in bad conditions." The plane wasn't rated to fly when the wind was above a certain speed, and Ruhl was damn sure it was close. Even on a good flying day, pontoons cause drag and wind can make flying with them hairy.

By the time Missy pulled into the gate Ruhl had left open and swung Silk's truck into the hangar, the snow was coming down steadily and the prop-wash was sucking swirls of it into the hangar around the plane. Missy stopped as near as she thought she should get to the plane, and helped Silk get Mac out of the back seat of the cab. The Cessna was idling, but when they got up next to it they realized the door on the pilot's side was open and there was no sign of Ruhl. Then a headlight cut through the snow and the snowplow Ruhl had driven down the taxiway and up the runway turned into the hangar. He parked the plow and ran back to assist Missy and Silk loading Mac into the plane.

Before he took off, over the sound of the propeller, Ruhl shouted that he was sure there was enough fuel to get to Juneau if they were lucky and conditions didn't force them out of their way. Daniel held Mac in his arms. The two of them squeezed into the second seat behind Ruhl. As Missy watched, Ruhl maneuvered the plane out of the hangar, down the taxiway, and around to the runway. Then it came barreling back in her direction. It was airborne before it passed her.

"I've never felt so helpless," Lea said when we had all gathered back at Leon's. We were waiting for the phone to ring, waiting to hear one thing and not another, waiting for the world to restore itself to order. Other people who had been on the march drifted into the café and Allison drained their largest coffee urn of the dregs from the morning and made another pot. No one said much. A few people who passed the table where I was sitting squeezed my shoulder when they came by. There were conversations, mostly muffled, mostly not for my ears, and I did my best to tune them out. I could not think about what was happening on that plane, or the fact that two of the people I was most connected to in the world were on it. Missy had used the satellite phone at the airport to call the air traffic in Juneau, and they promised a priority landing. Back in town, Sue-Ellen called the hospital. There was some official deference given to her as the town manager of Adolphus, but until they landed and Mac got transported to the hospital, there wasn't much anyone in Juneau could promise.

I kept thinking as I was sitting there what I would do if Mac was lost, or Allison or Lea or Missy or Ruhl. Or Rob. Or Sue-Ellen. Or Daniel Silk for that matter. These people were as close to family as I would likely have in my life between that moment and whenever it is done. Would I be able to stand being in Adolphus if any of them were suddenly taken away? I didn't want to entertain my blackest thoughts, but I couldn't seem to keep my mind from going there.

Outside, there was more than two inches of snow on the ground, and the rain underneath was now frozen. As people came in, they kept saying walking was treacherous. Everything felt treacherous to me. And in my mind's eye I kept seeing the plane flying into nothingness.

When the phone rang and Lea reported it was Ruhl on the line, the café erupted into cheers. But getting them there was only half the news. They had landed, but the plane was damaged, having skidded into a light standard on the icy runway and caromed off into a berm. No one was hurt, they hadn't been travelling very fast by that point, and Daniel Silk had Mac cradled in his arms and braced himself when they started to skid. The airport had been ready for them. An ambulance took Mac to the hospital, and Ruhl and Daniel, both of whom had some cuts and scratches, were treated by paramedics on the scene. Then Daniel had gone off somewhere. Ruhl didn't know where, but Silk had saluted him before walking away in the terminal, which Ruhl had taken to mean, "Job well done." Ruhl had saluted him back. Walt told Lea on the phone that he was headed to the hospital as well, if he could get a lift or a cab.

During the call, I noticed Rob had come in. He seemed to know what was going on, that his plane had been used, though I wasn't sure who told him. He was stoical. JoJo was at his side, the first time I had seen them together acting like a couple. He caught my eye across the room, nodded and lowered his eyes in a gesture of sympathy. I wondered if anyone's insurance was going to pay for the damage to the plane. Then Lea waved me over to the counter and said Ruhl wanted to talk to me.

"It doesn't look good," he told me after she handed me the phone. He was bad when we got here. I didn't want to say that to Lea to report to everyone, but you might want to see if there's another way to get here. I think it's possible he won't make it. Sorry to have to tell you."

"I'm not sure how."

"No. I know. Maybe someone here would be willing to fly over and get you. I can ask."

"That would be great. Let me know. Hey, Walt. I'm not going to tell people. I'm going to wait to hear what happens."

"Yea. That makes sense." After a moment he said, "I want to tell you, Silk was great. If Mac lives, he's why."

"I guess that means I'll have to give him a pass on his politics now."

"Yea. We owe him."

"I think you'll have had something to do with it, too, Walt." When I hung up, I felt like I could not draw a breath. Allison came over and put her arm around me.

"It'll be all right. He's a tough guy."

That night, before we knew what the long term was going be, but after Mac was in the hospital and we knew he was "stable," I went back to her place with Missy.

There were a lot of changes in Adolphus after that. It was as if the whole town got rejiggered in some way. I was taken to the hospital the next day. Ruhl persuaded an old friend to fly back across the Lynn and the Chilkats to pick me up. I got a hotel room and stayed by Mac's bedside for two weeks, telling him bad jokes, playing cards, and watching crappy TV.

When Mac was fully recovered, he moved back to New York, figuring he needed to be where there were better hospitals closer by, though we had gotten him to the emergency room in under an hour – no longer than it probably would have taken him to get across Manhattan on a bad gridlock day.

Before he moved away from Adolphus, during his recuperation, he got a lot of TLC from Lea and Allison. He took most of his meals at Leon's, and for the times they weren't open they made him things he could just heat up. Missy let him sit in for her at contract bridge, but he drove me crazy as a partner because he bid a lot of contracts he simple could never make. The four of us did a lot of laughing during those games. We knew he was going to move back east, but we delayed thinking about it until he was ready to go. Lea asked if they could have copies of some of his work to hang up in the café, and he arranged for high quality prints to be made and framed. "Now your café will be the most depressing place in Adolphus," he told them. "Dying polar bears, destroyed habitat, please to enjoy your pie." Allison told him, "There's beauty in the way you see, not just in what you see." He pretended she was full of shit, but I knew it meant a lot to him that she said that. No one said it aloud, but it was clear to me that Mac's days gallivanting off to Borneo and other far-flung places on assignment were probably over. He seemed to take it in stride, but I felt bad for him.

About three months after his heart attack, when he deemed himself recovered enough for some luxury domestic travel, he and I finally went to San Francisco together. It wasn't the trip we had planned, and we both knew it was kind of a goodbye, but we vowed to have a great time. Mac booked us into the Palace. We had rooms floors apart, but with the same view. I didn't resist his paying. He made it clear it was something he wanted to do. He should have done it for Walt and Daniel Silk as well.

The day we went to the San Francisco Fine Arts Museum, he picked up a woman. He was standing in front of David Wilkie's painting, *Bathsheba*. As Wilkie depicts her, Bathsheba is nude, sitting on a stool, slipping on a stocking. "You like your girls large?" the woman suddenly standing next to him in the otherwise empty gallery thirteen asked him. I overheard the conversation.

"That's a personal question," he answered before he turned.

He spent the next two nights with her, or rather, she spent them with him. She was what we would have called "ample" if we had been bullshitting in a bar somewhere,

196

though that was an opinion I never shared with him. It turned out she knew and loved Mac's wildlife shots. She was on vacation in San Francisco, but was the head of an endangered species protection foundation in New York City. The perfect pick up, the woman who got hot and bothered by his work. Her name was Monica Rothman. She and Mac were married in Manhattan in February 2004, on the anniversary of his heart attack. It was hell to get there, but I travelled four thousand miles to be his best man. Missy went with me.

I ended up sleeping with Missy the night of Mac's rescue. It was kind of an accident. We were sitting together on her couch waiting to hear if there was any more news about Mac's condition, and we nodded off with our heads on each other's shoulders. At some point she woke me and led me into her bedroom. Then I just never went home, and she never sent me.

Rob sold the plane back to Ruhl after it was repaired. It turned out Rob had insurance. Ruhl was back in the newspapers, but this time as a hero who took a big risk to save a friend. It was the kind of story Alaskans love to tell about themselves, man against the elements, man being defiant and brave. After some pressure from Sue-Ellen (wearing her town official hat), from our congressman, and eventually and reluctantly from the Governor, the FAA relented and provisionally reissued Ruhl's license, provided he never flew under the influence again. Rob kept up his bellyaching about how hard it was to stock the store in the winter, but Ruhl made some special trips for him now and then to pick up things that were over the weight allotment of the mail plane.

Jojo and Rob eventually got married and all the animosity about her leaving Burt Hull died down.

The day after Ruhl flew Mac to Juneau to catch his plane to New York, a package came to the café addressed to Allison. It was a CD of Eva Cassidy singing Louie

197

Armstrong's *It's a Wonderful World*, the closest Mac could get to replaying the sound of Allison's voice in his ear, his tribute.

Daniel Silk re-enlisted for Operation Iraqi Freedom a few months after his heroics in Adolphus. He was killed in late 2004 in Anbar Provence by a roadside IED. He had written a will before he shipped out. I'm told all active duty service personnel are required to do that. Much to her surprise, Silk left his truck to Missy Wiggins. She bombs around town in it, but is always mindful of her shifting. She wouldn't want to tear up Daniel's gears. I drive it now sometimes too, and never fail to think of him.

The story of our peace march had fairly long legs, as they call it in the news business. For whatever reason, the pictures Mac took of us, bundled against the cold, our ragtag line of march stretching out on the otherwise deserted Alaskan roadway, struck a chord. *The Times* printed Mac's pictures, taken moments before his collapse. At the big anti-war rally in Washington at the beginning of March, our picture, blown up to banner size, was hanging behind the speakers on the stage. Above it there was a sign that said, *"From Adolphus, Alaska, to Zion, Texas, the American people say 'No Invasion of Iraq.'"* I was in the center of the shot.

On March 19, 2003, the President authorized our military to unleash waves of bombs on Baghdad city. Within six weeks, over seven thousand Baghdadi citizens – neighbors, friends, lovers, grandparents, parents, and children – were dead. Shock and Awe.

ACKNOWLEDGEMENTS

To the people who have read and commented on these stories on their way to publication, I want to express my heartfelt thanks. These are: Diane Loebell, first and foremost, for being my first reader and diligent editor; the members of Working Writers Group, present and past, who encouraged and challenged me; Bonnie Gordon, whose thoughtful critique was invaluable at a crucial time; Leslie Rothman, for reading and archiving multiple drafts; pilots Jim Van Ness and Joe Capalbo for technical advice about flying; and finally, my colleagues and friends in the Philadelphia theater community, who have been long-term supporters of my literary and artistic endeavors. My gratitude.

41442261R00125

Made in the USA
Middletown, DE
13 March 2017